Bible Verses in my Pocket

Micah Stohlmann

Visit my website at www.bibleversesinmypocket.com

First printing: June 2011

ISBN-13: 978-0615481814

To my parents
Thanks for all the love and support.

Table of Contents

Chapter   Page

Introduction: Is There Time for the Word?   7

Chapter 1: Remembering the Word   25

Chapter 2: Direction from the Word   35

Chapter 3: The Word in My Pocket   50

Chapter 4: Love from the Word   66

Chapter 5: Life in the Word   86

Chapter 6: Service through the Word   102

Chapter 7: Staying in the Word   124

Conclusion: The Word is Life   148

Appendix   168

Sources   169

Introduction: Is There Time for the Word?

There is a time for everything, and a season for every activity under heaven.
Ecclesiastes 3:1

Take my time here on this earth
And let it glorify all that You are worth
For I am nothing
I am nothing without You
Lyrics from *Nothing Without You* by Bebo Norman[1]

"People only see what they are prepared to see."
Ralph Waldo Emerson

God's Word has the power to change lives. Through His gracious love Christians have a new life in Christ. However, in times of busyness, transition, and stress it can be hard to focus on anything but just getting through the day. Young adults in particular go through many transitions in life and often are busy attempting to start a career and a family. During young adulthood especially it seems that people take their faith for granted. However, God's Word is not just for part of a Christian's life it is a Christian's life. The benefits and blessings of being in God's Word and relying on him for guidance, strength, and hope throughout a believer's whole life are immeasurable. God has much to teach us and I guarantee that Christians will come to know wisdom beyond measure by being in His Word.

There are saying and phrases that are used a lot in society yet most people have forgotten where they came from or who said them first. A bird in the hand is worth two in the bush. A friend in need is a friend indeed. Better late than never. A house divided cannot stand. A picture's worth a thousand words. A penny for your thoughts. Buyer beware. A penny saved is a penny earned. The best things in life are free. Clothes may disguise a fool, but his voice will give him away. Beggars can't be choosers. Be careful what you wish for. You can lead a horse to water but you can't make him drink. You are what you eat.[2]

Have you ever heard the phrase "An elephant never forgets" and wondered where it comes from? Elephants have been known to recognize individual humans and other elephants after being separated for years. Elephants have also been observed to follow the exact same paths in their travels and even have the same burial places that they try to get back to if they know they are dying. The elephants seem to hand this down in their clans throughout their generations. There is a story called "elephant walk" in which the elephants, instead of walking around a British built villa, went right through it because it was in their traditional travel path.[3] Are there things that are that important in your family history that you would want to never forget?

Imagine that your family and community had been freed from slavery, rescued from recapture by the parting of a sea, been provided food for forty years in the desert, seen the walls of a strong castle collapse at the sound of trumpets, and conquered many kings and kingdoms that had more military power. How long would you remember, pass down the stories to your children, and praise the one that had done this for you. The Israelites had experienced this with God leading them into the Promised Land. Yet humans constantly forget the good things God has done for them. That is why we often need reminders such as the following. *When you have eaten and are satisfied, praise the Lord your God for the good land he has given you. Be careful that you do not forget the Lord your God. Deuteronomy 8: 10-11b.*

The book of Judges has a recurring cycle of the disobedience of Israel, foreign oppression, cries of distress and gracious divine deliverance. The book contrasts the unfaithfulness of Israel with the faithfulness and mercy of God.[4] Starting with Judges 2:11 the phrase, *the Israelites did evil in the eyes of the Lord*, is used six times in Judges. The Israelites had forgotten what God had done for them and had let their relationship with God slide. In God's mercy he raised up judges to help the people of Israel and remind them of their Savior. Othniel, Ehud, Deborah, Gideon, Jephthah, and Samson are the major judges mentioned. The judges were able to remind the Israelites that God was their king and that they should repent of their evil ways. Remembering what God had done to save them and returning to God's love allowed the Israelites to have peace and security. God's faithfulness and patience is demonstrated in His forgiveness of the repeated disobedience of the Israelites.

Are people today any different from the Israelites? Overall 45% of people in the U.S. never or seldom attend church.[5] Youth groups in churches are often filled with middle school and high school children. However, it is often the case that after high school graduation many of these young people attend church less frequently. My experiences in life have lead me to notice that the age range of people with the least frequent church attendance are young adults. A recent Gallup poll found that 35% of people age 18 to 29 attend church weekly or almost weekly.[5] This was the smallest percentage of any age range listed.

No one but God can judge the true faith of an individual. So, while church attendance by itself is not a measure of faith the question still remains as to why this age group does not attend church often. There are great benefits from worshiping and fellowshipping with a community of believers that are being missed.

Young adulthood involves many changes and new experiences. Young adults are trying to start a career, get married, start a family, and many other first time experiences. The busyness and transitions during this time of life can leave no room for God. So He is often pushed to the side.

Besides lack of church attendance there is other evidence that too many young adults in the U.S. take their faith in God for granted. A survey of 18 to 29 year olds done by LifeWay found encouraging information in that 65% of those surveyed called themselves Christians. However, the survey also indicated that some of the respondents who called themselves Christians did not see their faith as a large part of their life. Of the respondents that said that they will go to heaven because Jesus Christ is their Savior, 68% did not mention their faith or religion when asked what was really important in their life. Fifty percent of these respondents did not attend church weekly, 36% rarely or never read the Bible, and only 40% thought it was their responsibility to share the Gospel with others.[6]

Non-Christian young adults are being impacted and have noticed the attitudes of Christian young adults. National survey research of non-Christians age 16 to 29 done by the Barna Group revealed how non-Christians viewed Christianity. They found that 84% of non-Christians knew a Christian personally. However, only 15% of non-Christians that knew a Christian felt that there was a lifestyle difference in the way their Christian friends lived.[7]

A result of this is that non-Christians have a view of Christianity that is not completely accurate. The Barna Group survey found that Non-Christian young adults think that Christians are judgmental, insensitive, do not show love to others, and are out of touch with today's culture.[7] This is further support that Christian young adults have problems remembering what God has done for them in Christ and how this should affect their lives.

What can be done to help young adults not forget their faith in God? This book will focus on answering this question. I felt the problem of being busy in my life during my college years and the years following. I have also experienced the problem of forgetting to live out my faith.

While adjusting to the transitions of young adulthood I have also struggled with a chronic illness. My hope is that others can learn through my experiences of how the Word of God has impacted my life. This book seeks to show that the power of the Word of God is real and can provide guidance, wisdom, comfort, hope and joy in the life of a Christian.

The idea for writing this book came from God speaking to me through His Word. For the past 25 months I have been carrying around Bible verses on a sheet in my pocket. Keeping Bible verses in my pocket has helped me to learn from God daily and keep my life in prospective. Daily meditation on God's Word allows Christians to be strengthened by God throughout the day.

My Story of Transition

In my everyday life there are often times I get busy and fail to remember both major things as well as minor ones. At times it is hard for me to focus on taking time for others because of my type A personality. I have a planner that I use to write down appointments or things that I have to do. I have found that if I do not write things down it is too easy to forget. Every day I usually have a list of things that I want to get done. I consider myself an organized person and it is a point of pride that I do not get caught off guard or easily forget things. When I end up being late or forgetting something, it can be very frustrating.

In college I was a resident assistant and supposed to be in the know about all campus activities. One February morning I woke up and began the process of getting ready for my 8:30 class on Lutheran Confessional Heritage. There had been a lot of snow the previous night and some talk about classes being cancelled. On my way to the shower I noticed a sign on the door that led to the dorm exit. It was written in marker and stated that all classes were cancelled today due to snow. I excitedly headed back to my room and told three other students on my floor that there were no classes today. In hindsight the sign having been written in marker should have been a clue that something was not right; but whether it was wishful thinking or the early morning I proceeded back to my room and went to sleep.

I woke up several hours later, like a bear out of winter hibernation, and decided I should get something to eat. I bundled up and went outside and noticed some friends walking back to the dorm with their backpacks. I thought it was strange and asked if they had been studying in the library. They looked at me oddly and said that they were coming back from class. I discovered later that one of my friends had posted signs around the building as a joke and did not think that anyone would actually fall for them. Sometimes being prepared is no match for a well-placed sign.

Moving forward eight years, I was still learning to pay attention to what is important. It was April fool's day in 2008. I had been in the hospital since the night before and had been waiting all day for the doctor to talk to me about what he thought he would do. I spent a lot of time in prayer; talking to God during the day. It was now towards the evening and they were prepping me for surgery. I knew that I probably had an infection from inflammation of my intestine that had to be dealt with but did not know what else would happen. The doctor arrived and basically told me the same thing; that they would cut me open but were not sure exactly what they would find. It was no joke. I was about to have major surgery. .

Taking time to slow down the pace of life and keep all things in perspective is a valuable life skill that I am working on. Mahatma Gandhi had a saying that "there is more to life than increasing its speed." In college I was involved in football and choir, which were time consuming commitments. During college I also had a number of jobs that I worked. In addition to being a resident assistant; I worked as a campus security guard, math tutor, and worked with two developmentally disabled adults. I did not have as much time to socialize as other college students but I thrived on being busy. The jobs were fun and allowed me to meet a number of different people.

I have found that life often has unexpected occurrences and does not always go as I plan. While I was in choir my senior year of college we went on a tour through California and Arizona. When we were in Los Angeles, I remember looking over the endless stretch of houses and buildings crammed together like too many people in a phone booth. I said to myself that I could never live here. Humans might make plans but sometimes God has other plans. You might guess what ended up happening towards the end of the summer. I accepted a call to teach at a Lutheran high school in the San Fernando Valley ten minutes from Los Angeles!

In my first teaching job I kept busy as I had during my college years. It was a small school and each grade had only around seventeen students. While I was there I taught mathematics and physical education classes. In addition to teaching responsibilities I was the athletic director, coached sports, and helped out backstage in our school's musical production of *How to Succeed in Business*. Being involved with the church that was connected to the school also brought more opportunities including working with the youth group and being a member of the board of the church. I quickly learned that not teaching during the summer is necessary for teachers to recharge.

After teaching for two years in Los Angeles, I felt the need to further my education so I returned to Minnesota and attended the University of Minnesota to get my masters in mathematics education. I kept a similar busy lifestyle during this time. While going to school fulltime, I worked fulltime at a retail clothing store and at athletic events on campus. It was an intense year and a half. Everyday I was at least working eight hours of the day or going to classes; sometimes both. When I finished my masters program in December, I was a long-term substitute teacher for two months. After this I just worked part time and started applying for teaching jobs for the new school year ahead. It was nice to have some rest, because I was definitely approaching burn out. Like the runners after crossing the finish line at the Ironman triathlon in Hawaii, I felt exhaustion and relief.

However, in the extra free time that I had I did not always make good choices of what to do. I went out with friends to bars and drank too much alcohol about once or twice a week. At the time I felt that drinking alcohol allowed me to have a better time and enjoy life. Looking back it at it now it seems stupid, but at the time my focus in life was not completely centered on my relationship with God. *I tried cheering myself with wine, and embracing folly—my mind still guiding me with wisdom. I wanted to see what was worthwhile for men to do under heaven during the few days of their lives. Ecclesiastes 2:3* The author of Ecclesiastes went through a similar experience as he looks back on his life and realize what is most important. He states throughout the book that life that is not centered on God is purposeless and meaningless.

Up to this point in my life I had been shy when approaching or talking to women. Alcohol allowed me to have more confidence and talk more freely. But when I was drinking I was not the person that I wanted to be or who I knew that I was in Christ. Solomon notes the folly of over indulging in alcohol. *Wine is a mocker and beer a brawler; whoever is led astray by them is not wise. Proverbs 20:1* I needed to refocus my life and draw my strength and self-confidence from my relationship with God.

Research consistently shows that people tend to drink the heaviest in their late teens and early to mid-twenties, which can cause damaging effects to their lives. Alcohol consumption is the third leading preventable cause of death in the United States.[8] The misuse of alcohol can also lead to alcohol poisoning, unintentional injuries, violence, depression, risky behaviors, and damaged relationships. It is important for Christians to help others so that they do not abuse alcohol. Christians can show others a better way to live life through their actions and words.

At the end of the summer I was able to land a job at a large public high school. It was a much different teaching experience than my previous one. The number of students in the school was twenty times larger than my previous job and I was teaching three to four times as many students during the day.

During the school year I moved into a house where four of my friends were living. Growing up I had two brothers and two sisters so I was used to living with others. However, anyone that has lived with friends knows that you learn some interesting things about your friends when you share a residence. Our definitions of what clean was were polar opposites. I believed in cleaning weekly and they felt cleaning should be done as often as your taxes. This too took some adjusting. While teaching I coached basketball during the school year, which meant that I was at school close to twelve hours most days. It ended up making my body wear down on April fool's day in 2008.

Crohn's disease was an anomaly that I had not heard of until 2000. Crohn's disease is a chronic disorder that causes inflammation of the digestive or gastrointestinal tract. It is similar to ulcerative colitis and both involve an abnormal response by the body's immune system. One of the jobs of the immune system is to protect the body from infection. Crohn's disease can cause a person's immune system to react inappropriately and cause inflammation. There are about one million Americans with Crohn's disease or ulcerative colitis.[9]

In 2000 I was diagnosed with Crohn's disease after having problems with a couple of cysts during the summer. My local doctor did not know what was wrong and I ended up being able to see a specialist at the University of Minnesota just in time for surgery. The previous two nights I was unable to sleep as intense pain kept me awake. One of the nights I attempted to watch Indiana Jones and the Last Crusade at three in the morning to help put me to sleep. It did not work but it helped me feel Harrison Ford's pain as he fought his way through the movie. When I finally got into the doctor at the University of Minnesota he noticed a cyst, which they ended up cutting open and draining. By the time they did the surgery it had mushroomed to the size of a baseball and my temperature was a boiling one hundred and four degrees.

Up until 2008 I had been in relative good health and had no further problems from my Crohns. Having had surgery on April fool's 2008 was something that was not funny at the time but I can look back now and joke about the irony. I had been a fool for not taking better care of myself. I had been feeling sick and tired for about a couple weeks leading up to April the first. The night before, I had gone into the doctor's office with severe abdominal pain and they did a CT scan. The results of the test informed the doctor that I had to be in the hospital.

This brings me back to the beginning of my story as I was being prepared for surgery. As the doctor was administering anesthesia I felt like a fool for another reason. Not wanting to worry my family I had called only my older brother and told him that I was in the hospital. He did not know that I was going to have surgery. When the anesthesia was kicking in, I remember thinking that no one knows that I am about to undergo surgery.

Repeating a couple Bible verses during the day and before the surgery had given me comfort knowing that God was with me no matter what the outcome. *For I know the plans I have for you, declares the Lord, plans to prosper you and not to harm you, plans to give you hope and a future. Jeremiah 29:11 And we know that in all things God works for the good of those who love him, who have been called according to his purpose. Romans 8:28* It was a relief to wake up from the surgery and see family members. I was hooked up to a number of different machines, had twenty-four staples to keep my six inch incision closed but was glad to be through the surgery.

The recovery was a long process. The surgery had entailed a bowel resection of damaged parts of my small and large intestine, the clearing of an infection, removal of my appendix, and the removal of a carcinoid tumor. The surgery was a long process. The doctor made sure to check that I did not have any cancer by testing twenty three of my lymph nodes. Surprisingly to me at the time, the day after surgery I felt like I would be back to teaching the next week. I had not even got out of bed yet or eaten anything besides liquids. At the time I did not realize that the painkillers were making me feel a lot better than I was. Once I started to wean off painkillers and move around it was a different story. It was like looking at a couch and thinking you could carry it up a flight of stairs; only to realize that when you try to lift it you cannot even pick the couch up. After six weeks I was able to go back to teaching and was still feeling pretty weak. During the six weeks of recovery I spent another week in the hospital when an infection reoccurred near my bowel resection site. In all I had lost thirty five pounds over the six weeks and felt like a shadow of my former self.

Through it all I was able to stay optimistic by knowing that God is with me always. *So do not fear, for I am with you; do not be dismayed, for I am your God. I will strengthen you and help you; I will uphold you with my righteous right hand. Isaiah 41:10.* My relationship with God was a great comfort in my illness. It has not only been essential in my tough times but has been valuable in times of joy and successes as well. I know that any talent or gifts I have are from God, as well as any good that results from them.

In my relationship with God I know that He will be teaching me more as the years go by. *Your word is a lamp to my feet and a light for my path. Psalm 119: 105.* God's Word can provide direction when life decisions become unclear. About a year later I found myself in the hospital again and it was another learning experience from God. What I learned will be discussed more in a later chapter.

No matter what problems or challenges one may have in a day; taking time to slow down and start it with God can put the rest of the day in perspective. Making sure to remember that I am a redeemed child of God helps me let the love of Christ show in all my decisions, and can lead to less stress and a more fulfilling day. *I have hidden your word in my heart that I might not sin against you. Psalm 119:11*

Psalm 119 is the longest Psalm in the Bible containing 176 verses. The verses are divided into sections of eight verses. If you read through the sections you will notice a common theme. The author is focused on the Word of God for all moments in life. The author relies on God's Word for guidance, trust, grace, hope, comfort, praise, joy, love, preservation, understanding, and safety. The author appears to have had a tough life. *My comfort in my suffering is this: Your promise preserves my life. Psalm 119:50* However, the author relies on God's Word for continued support.

The Bible has wisdom to enable Christians to cope with any situation in life. God desires to be in our whole life, not just when we feel we need help. God wants to communicate and build a relationship with each of us. When

I am daily in God's Word I know it will always be in my heart and on my mind. This leads me to discuss my faith with others. Then God does great things in my life and in the lives of others.

What are some ways that this can be accomplished in the midst of our busy days and unending "to do" lists? Paul writes in 1 Thessalonians 5:17 to pray continually and in verses 21 and 22 to hold on to the good and avoid every kind of evil. To pray continually means that in our daily tasks we can direct our unspoken thoughts to God trusting in His promise to hear and answer.

When we are weak God's strength supports and sustains us. *My grace is sufficient for you, for my power is made perfect in weakness. Therefore I will boast all the more gladly about my weaknesses, so that Christ's power may rest on me. 2 Corinthians 12:9* The apostle Paul wrestled with a weakness which he called his "thorn in the flesh." No one knows for sure what this thorn in his flesh really represented. However, he found that because of it's presence, he was much more aware of the power of God at work in his life. Paul's trust in God's promise to help enabled him to endure many sufferings for the sake of the Gospel. Being able to communicate with God daily in prayer can help us also endure our life's painful experiences and celebrate life's joys.

I felt the problem of being too busy in my life, not taking enough time for others, and feeling like there was too much to do. The idea for this book, *Bible Verses in My Pocket*, helps me to keep my mind and heart focused on things above. Whether it is taking time for devotions or prayer throughout the day, being involved in a Bible study, having friends or family remind you of God's love, or saying a short prayer for everyone you meet God's Word is too important not to keep in your heart and mind.

In Deuteronomy, Moses stresses the importance of remembering the Word of God to the Israelites. *These commandments that I give you today are to be upon your hearts. Impress them on your children. Talk about them when you sit at home and when you walk along the road, when you lie down and when you get up. Tie them as symbols on your hands and bind them on your foreheads. Deuteronomy 6: 6-8 Fix these words of mine in your hearts and minds. Deuteronomy 11:18a* Like many people today, the Israelites needed reminders to not take their relationship with God for granted.

What events and times in your daily life are opportunities to spend time in God's Word? Compared to forty years ago Americans have 45 more minutes of leisure time each day.[10] On average each day Americans spend four and a half hours watching television,[11] are exposed to 61 minutes of TV ads and promotions,[12] and spend 45 to 60 minutes waiting.[13] Daily there are times when I found that I would have to wait or have a couple minutes before I had to do something else. We can use these times to remember what is important in life. During these times, at the bank, at the grocery store, while cooking food, waiting for a friend, waiting for a class to start, waiting for a meeting, during commercials on TV; I reach into my pocket and spend some time in God's Word.

Chapter 1: Remembering the Word

Let the word of Christ dwell in you richly as you teach and admonish one another with all wisdom, and as you sing psalms, hymns and spiritual songs with gratitude in your hearts to God.
Colossians 3:16

"When you see God's hand in everything, it is easy to put everything in God's hands"
Unknown Author

The human mind and body is a marvel of God's creation. How even the smallest cell is so complex is proof of God's handiwork. The brain is an amazing instrument and can hold vasts amount of information. However, humans have a tendency to forget things over time. Reading, reviewing, and discussing God's Word will enable it to be written on our hearts and to be used daily in life for guidance, encouragement, and hope.

It is said the very best in their field have so much experience and knowledge that they have forgotten more than most people will ever learn. Even with what has been forgotten they still have immense knowledge. Several years ago there was a newspaper story about a man that had worked the same job for sixty years. Tom Triemert celebrated his sixtieth year of working at Strauss Knitting Mills in St. Croix Falls, Wisconsin in 2007. Tom has seen and learned a lot in those years but defines his philosophy as this; "I think you gotta lay back and don't get excited. Don't get too hard on people, and don't be too hard on yourself, either." With all of those years logged at work one of his hobbies is still knitting; which he does to donate caps to the poor.[1] Tom has probably forgotten more about how the Knitting mills factory works then others know about the company.

It is natural for people to forget things throughout their life. Some things are unimportant details and others are more significant things that should be remembered. Christians want to make sure that they keep in mind what God has done and continues to do for them in their life. Reading God's Word can help Christians to remember what He has done for them. James chapter 1:22-26 talks about how Christians that read God's Word, do not forget it, and put it into practice will be blessed in what they do.

If you look in the mirror and walk away, do you immediately forget what you look like? Why then do Christians so often read the Bible and immediately forget its message? A person could leave a church service and on the drive home yell at someone they think is driving too slow. How can people deal with this tendency to forget?

Teachers are always looking for ways for their students to have longer retention of concepts. When I was a high school mathematics teacher, I attended a workshop on collaboration. Part of the information that the presenter talked about was the top three brain grabbers to get students to learn and retain information. Take a second and think back to when you were in school and think of a teacher that really got you to excel. See if you can recall what it was about this teacher that made him or her excellent.

My guess is they used one or all of these three things. The first one was novelty. If something is new or exciting a person will be involved and be interested more. Second was movement. Simply doing something with your hands or any movement can keep people alert and awake. For example, trying to learn how to play tennis by listening to someone talk for a day would lead to boredom and frustration. People need to try something to learn it properly. Third was emotional intensity. People must feel a connection and have genuine interest in what they are doing to really stimulate brain activity. These three brain grabbers will work with people of any age.

What people remember can be affected by what they feel is important. Paul offers advice on what Christians can focus on during a day. *Let the word or Christ dwell in you richly as teach and admonish one another with all wisdom. Colossians 3:16* What do you feel is important to focus on during the day?

Motivation for Remembering the Word

Growing up in Lutheran schools all the way through college I had memory verses to recite and write out. I remember wondering in sixth grade about when I would not have to memorize Bible verses for class. I did not completely understand the point of having verses memorized and being able to meditate on the Word of God.

There is infinite wisdom in the Bible that God can use to teach Christians their whole lives. No one can ever completely understand and have answers to all faith questions except Jesus. As I grow older I know with many things I know only a little and may never fully understand them. 1 Corinthians 13:12 states this *"Now we see but a poor reflection as in a mirror, then we shall see face to face. Now I know in part; then I shall know fully, even as I am fully known."*

College is often the time when people realize that there is a lot that they do not know. When I was in college I took a class from my dad called Our Living Faith. Part of the class was memorizing verses from Scripture. It was valuable and I came to appreciate and really understand the meaning of having the Word on my heart.

Being interested in a topic, visualizing it, relating to it, and repeating it can lead to better memory. The pieces of Scripture I had to memorize for the class connect easily with these memory aids. One of the passages was Psalm 1. It talks directly to the way of the sinners and the way of the righteous. The verses have great imagery and can be visualized easily. The **righteous** are *like a tree planted by streams of water, which yields its fruit in season and whose leaf does not wither. Whatever they do prospers. Not so the **wicked!** They are **like chaff** that the wind blows away. Therefore the wicked **will not stand** in the judgment nor sinners in the assembly of the righteous. Psalm 1:3-5*

It is easy to relate to these verses, which speak to what will happen to the righteous and what will happen to the wicked. The wicked are easily swayed and have no foundation; even a light wind can blow them away. On the other hand the righteous have a strong foundation in God and yield much fruit. They are spiritually healthy.

The motivation to be in God's Word comes from what He has done for us and the Holy Spirit at work in a person's life. It is not because the Bible verses are interesting, visual and applicable; though they are. God sent Jesus to die on the cross for our sins. Because of this Christians are declared righteous and free from the condemnation of sin. The love that God has shown us motivates us to grow closer to Him. Christians can rely on the Holy Spirit for guidance when studying God's Word.

The other Bible memory verses that were part of the course to be memorized were Psalm 19:1-4, Romans 2:14-16, 2 Timothy 3:14-17, Psalm 8, Psalm 130, Romans 8:31-39, Galatians 5:16, 22-26, Ephesians 4:1-6, and Ephesians 2:19-22. They contain valuable wisdom that can help one witness to others, give advice, help or counsel a friend through tough times, or just be daily encouragement. Having Bible verses for these occasions can be a great help.

In the hymnals in my home church there was a red bookmark that had specific Bible verses for comfort, anger, jealousy, grief, depression, joy, celebration, thanksgiving and more. For any mood or occasion there is wisdom and guidance in the Bible. It is a true compassion story of God's never ending love for us that plays out in all of our lives.

Sometimes in church I would hear a good Bible verse

on Sunday that related to what I was going through in life and found relevant to my current situation. It would stay with me only for a couple of days though and then with the busyness of life I would forget it's message. I was missing the daily meditation on the word and the conversation with others about it that would keep my focus and vision on what God wants for my life.

Jesus' use of the Word

During his time on earth Jesus set the example for how Christians can keep the Word in their mind and heart.[2] He often would refer to Scriptures so that He would have an answer for anyone who doubted the power and truth of God. *Always be prepared to give an answer to everyone who asks you to give the reason for the hope that you have. But do this with gentleness and respect. 1 Peter 3:15.* When Jesus was tempted in the desert after fasting for forty days, He responded to the temptations with scripture. *Jesus answered him, "It is written: 'Do not put the Lord your God to the test.'" Matthew 4:7.* Jesus was quoting from Deuteronomy 6:16.

Jesus example was demonstrated even further in his last hours on the cross. When His suffering and pain was the worst and Jesus felt that God was far from him, he still turned to Scripture. *An at the ninth hour Jesus cried out in a loud voice, "Eloi, Eloi, lama sabachthani?" which means, "My God, my God, why have you forsaken me?" Mark 15:33-34.* At this point Jesus felt far from God. In our own lives if it seems that God is far from us we can know that he will never leave us. We can follow Jesus example if we will feel that God is not with us and our suffering is too much to bear. Jesus words on the cross were from Psalm 22:1. *My God, my god, why have you forsaken me? Why are you so far from saving me, so far from the words of my groaning?* When Jesus was in his toughest hour he still relied on the Scriptures.

Not only did he turn to Scriptures but he prayed to God. In our lives we can turn to Bible verses that we have memorized for any moment of our lives. We can also pray to God and lay all of our petitions before him. Like a loving father, God wants to hear our requests and concerns. Jesus last words on the cross showed that his trust in God his Father was not shaken. *Jesus called out with a loud voice, "Father, into your hands I commit my spirit." When he had said this, he breathed his last. Luke 23: 46* Again Jesus was quoting Scripture, Psalm 31:5, and communicating with God.

Another lesson to be learned from Jesus in this verse is that when we rely on the Word of God, have Bible verses on our heart, and pray to God then we can have rest in God's loving arms. Jesus was at peace before his death. He knew that the devil had been defeated and that in three days He would rise victorious having paid for all of our sins. *He is not here; he has risen, just as he said. Come and see the place where he lay. Matthew 28:6* Christians can have peace knowing that Jesus is our Savior. He has defeated death and redeemed us.

Phil Stacey has a song called "You're Not Shaken" that describes how we can be comforted by what Jesus has done for us on the cross. *When I am in the valley of the shadow* of death. *You're not shaken, You're not shaken. You're right here beside me and You have never left.*[3] Christians can look to the love of Jesus for comfort and strength in life.

Calling of the Cross

Christians can look to the cross in their relationships with God to understand the depth of God's love and power. *For the message of the cross is foolishness to those who are perishing, but to us who are being save it is the power of God. 1 Corinthians 1:18* Jesus death and resurrection allows the Christian life to be a daily dying and rising with Christ. Christians know that we are sinners but with God's power and forgiveness the punishment of our sins can be removed. Jesus also said that we must carry our own crosses or burdens in this life with complete dedication and willing obedience to God, recorded in Luke 9:23. *If anyone would come after me, he must deny himself and take up his cross daily and follow me.* As well as in Luke 14:27, *and anyone who does not carry his cross and follow me cannot be my disciple.*

There is a movie called, *The Cross,*[4] that tells the story of Arthur Blessitt who followed these words of Jesus in his ministry around the world. For forty years starting in 1969 Arthur walked around every country in the world carrying a twelve-foot cross and telling others of the power of Jesus' love. He walked over 38,000 miles over the forty years. It is a miracle in itself that he survived walking through war zones, Iran, North Korea, and managed to keep from getting sick. He did not always know where he would get food and water.

In the movie Arthur comments that people know that they have problems, they know that they are not perfect, and they are looking for a way out. Arthur came to find that the people in the worst and most difficult places are the ones that welcome the cross the most. In Christ, people can become a new creation. *Therefore, if anyone is in Christ, he is a new creation; the old has gone, the new has come! 2 Corinthians 5:17* When people accept God's redeeming love, they are new people. They are no longer sinners but saints.

Sometimes people can feel that others do not know what they have gone through or where they are from. In the movie Arthur starts a conversation with a man on the street. "I've been through your country." The man replies "Oh yeah, well how do you know where I'm from?" Arthur responds, "I don't know where you are from but I've been through every nation in the world." The message of the cross is that Jesus knows where everyone is from and what everyone has done. At the cross the worst of humans meet the best of God. *Praise the Lord, O my soul, and forget not all his benefits—who redeems your life from the pit and crowns you with love and compassion. Psalm 103:2,4* Jesus in his death on the cross has paid for the sins of the world. He rose from the dead and achieved victory for all of us.

Christians can tell about how their relationship with God has given them meaning and purpose for life. The song lyrics of "Because He Lives" by Bill Gaither[5] are a fitting description of what Christians can keep in mind in their daily life because of Jesus resurrection.

> *Because He lives, I can face tomorrow*
> *Because He lives, all fear is gone;*
> *Because I know He holds the future,*
> *And life is worth the living,*
> *Just because He lives!*

He is risen! Alleluia! Praise is raised. Jesus lifts us out of our bondage to death. *God made him who had no sin to be sin for us, so that in him we might become the righteousness of God. 2 Corinthians 5:21* If God can raise Jesus from the dead, He can help us in any of life's occurrences. You do not have to bear your burdens alone. He can take away all of your fears. So today rejoice and celebrate; Jesus is no longer dead but alive. He is alive and is risen indeed! This good news is too significant not to keep in our hearts and minds. Jesus set an example for how Bible verses can help us and remind us that God will never leave us. In the midst of the busyness of life when we may have to remember to do many things during the day; what greater daily task is there than to have the Word of God on our hearts and minds? A God that did not spare his own son but gave him up to death that we might all share in eternal life in heaven is definitely good news worth remembering.

Chapter 2: Direction from the Word

I will lead the blind by ways they have not known, along unfamiliar paths I will guide them; I will turn the darkness into light before them and make the rough places smooth. These are the things I will do; I will not forsake them.
Isaiah 42:16

"Once you learn how to die, you learn how to live."
Morrie Schwartz

What would you like to know about the future? There are many questions that come to mind when people are going through transitions in life. Will I get the job I interviewed for? How will I pay the rent and put food on the table? Who will I marry? Should I go back to school? Is it time to have children? Christians do not know what the future holds, but they do know who holds the future. No matter what twists and turns life can take, God is with us and His Word provides focus and meaning in life.

As I am writing this I am currently watching my parent's dog for three days. My parents are having work done on their house and needed someone to watch their dog. He is the dog that my family had since my junior year of high school. He is a Springer Spaniel Beagle mix, who is white with black spots, and is a true hound. His name is

Lucky[v] and he truly is. He has survived eating a whole pan of brownies when the vet thought he would not make it through the night.

He is thirteen years old and unfortunately mostly blind now. He has become cautious of new surroundings and no longer romps like a young puppy for fear of running into things. He is still content and happy though. He is never happier than when he gets to take walks. The comfort and assurance of being on a leash and knowing that he will be guided by someone that loves and cares for him let him move faster and not worry about his blindness. Knowing that someone you trust has your direction for your life in his or her hands is a comforting thought.

A couple years ago my parents were having work done on the outside of the house. Lucky was in the fenced in backyard. The workers had accidentally left the gate open and Lucky figured it would be a good time to sniff around in the front yard. He must have started walking and was not able to find his way back before anyone noticed that he was gone.

My mom, my brother and I started to comb the area to see where he could have gone. Finally after about forty minutes of searching Lucky was found cornered on the porch of someone's house about a mile from home. The man who owned the house had noticed Lucky wandering

---

[v] : People or places marked with a v in the book have videos available to watch that provide further information. The YouTube web address is given in the sources at the end of the book.

around, thought he was in danger, and had got him on his porch and made sure that he stayed there. It was a huge relief. When we got Lucky to my parent's house it was obvious that he too was happy to be home.

It is a fitting illustration of what can happen to Christians. Like Lucky, sometimes our **spiritual blindness** can cause us to stray too far off the path. We wander far from the person who is leading and watching out for us. If the gate is left open we might think we will just wander around a little bit to experiment. This can lead to many problems and setbacks. As well as a feeling of despair when we realize that we do not know where we are going.

When Christians stray from God, there is still unconditional love waiting for us. At times in life it may seem to people that all is lost. However, God can use others, His Word, and sacraments to show His steadfast love. Christians can be confident that they are never lost or alone because God will never leave us.

Believers are found

Sometimes people wander aimlessly when they do not find what they are looking for in life. They feel that purpose is missing in their life. They lack a feeling of peace and contentment. Christians find that sense of peace and contentment in God's promises and direction for their lives. *For it is by grace you have been saved, through faith– and this not from yourselves, it is the gift of God– not by works, so that no one can boast. For we are God's workmanship, created in Christ Jesus to do good works, which God prepared in advance for us to do.*

Ephesians 2:8-10 Relying on God's grace and knowing that our faith is not dependent on any works that we have done helps to put life in perspective. Eternal life and faith are gifts from God based on his unconditional love for us. God's love is pure and self-sacrificing.

The band U2 in 1987 came out with a song called *I still haven't found what I'm looking for* that describes a person that is searching for direction and fulfillment in life. The song ends with, I still haven't found what I'm looking for.[1] Many who do not know Jesus adopt this view and continue searching for what Jesus has to offer. They find meaning, direction, and purpose in life elsewhere. Christians know that Jesus has broken the bonds of sin for us and carried the cross and our shame by dying and rising again for us. With that great comfort Christians can proclaim that they have found what they're looking for. The great hope of Christians is that the last line of the song could be changed and everyone in the world could say that they have found what they are looking for in Jesus as their Lord and Messiah. The refrain from the hymn "Lift High the Cross" puts it nicely. *Lift high the cross, the love of Christ proclaim. Till all the world adore his sacred name.*

When my mom, brother, and I got Lucky back home I have never seen a dog wag his tail so much and be so happy to be home. Lucky had ventured out on his own and realized that that was not where he belonged. He was now home and happy. That night Lucky slept better than he had in a long time. He had a sense of peace and safety.

Christians know that if we listen to God's direction for our life and rely on His grace then we can have peace and safety in God's loving arms. *I will instruct you and teach you in the way you should go; I will counsel you and watch over you. Psalm 32:8*

God's responses to prayer

How can Christians know if they are listening to God's direction for their lives? People make thousands of decisions everyday. Think about how many decisions you have to make just to get ready in the morning. You have to decide what time to wake up, how long to shower, how long to brush your teeth, what to wear, what to eat for breakfast, what to do with your hair, what time to leave, and many other decisions. Many little decisions do not have a long lasting effect on a person's life and mistakes in these decisions can be quickly corrected. In big life decisions it can be harder to know what to do. However, in all of our decisions we can keep in mind that God wants us to give glory to Him in all that we do. By what we wear, what we say, how we treat others, and how we take care of God's creation we can give glory to God.

My parents' dog Lucky can listen and follow directions with certain commands. Lucky knows how to "stay", "come", "sit", and "go back". When Lucky comes back from walks and it has been raining he has muddy paws. He knows that when he is told to "stay" he needs to remain on the welcome mat until someone gets a towel to wipe his feet off. He also knows how to "come". When he is out in the back yard, he knows he can listen to the voice of my mom or dad when they say "Lucky come" to help him find the door. A trick that my Dad likes to do with Lucky involves my Dad putting a treat on the floor in front of Lucky when he is sitting. Lucky knows that he should not go anywhere because he just has to "sit" long enough to be able to be allowed to eat the treat. Lucky learned "go back" by getting his nose in places that it did not belong. Sometimes he will try to sniff all the way inside the refrigerator when it is open. He is quickly told to "go back".

When we pray to God for guidance, He answers by asking for similar responses from us. God may say, "stay" or "wait" in answer to our prayer request. People might want something in their life or desire a change. People suffering illnesses often pray for a quick recovery and a return to normal life. However, people often have to deal with various ailments in their lives that do not always have a quick remedy. Christians know that they can communicate to God in these difficult times. They can also find that God can work good out of what we perceive as a bad situation.

In writing this book I felt a strong desire to have a publisher after three months of writing. It was disappointing when I was unable to get a publisher. However, I came to realize that I needed to put more work into this book. God still had a lot to teach me that I could share with others. People may want something really bad and God does not say no, but just now is not the right time. Down the road the change may happen but for now God wants us to continue to persevere and trust in His love.

God may say, "come". The answer to our prayer request can be yes. God may grant our request or give us reassurance on a decision. This could involve reassurance on deciding to move to a new city or to switch jobs. God can provide peace of mind that we should proceed with the change.

God may say, "sit". This is equivalent to an answer of no to a prayer request. Examples could be if people are asking for fame, riches, popularity or a promotion. When God answers "no" we can trust that His answer is good for us. *I am the Lord your God, who teaches you what is best for you, who directs you in the way you should go. Isaiah 48:17b*

God may say, "go back". This answer indicates that we have in some way wandered from following His will in our lives. Through His Word God seeks to call us back to His will for our life. "Go back" means we need to refocus our priorities in life. Repentance is a necessary part of such refocusing. *"Even now," declares the Lord, "return to me with all your heart, with fasting and weeping and mourning." Rend your heart and not your garments. Return to the Lord your God, for he is gracious and compassionate, slow to anger and abounding in love Joel 2:12-13* Heartfelt repentance is not easy. So the prophet Joel reminds us that the nature of God abounds in grace and compassion.

An active prayer life, which obeys these divine commands, is a powerful way to communicate with God.

Such a prayer life that listens for God's answers helps provide direction and purpose in our daily lives. God can communicate wisdom to Christians through His Word and other Christians.

Studying God's Word for Guidance

Solomon is often said to be one of the wisest people to ever live. Many people came to him for advice. Solomon knew that his wisdom came from God. At the beginning of his reign God asked him to say whatever he wanted and it would be given to him. Solomon did not ask for fame or wealth but wisdom and was blessed in many ways. *The blessing of the Lord brings wealth, and He adds no trouble to it. Proverbs 10:22* The wisdom that comes from God is priceless and beyond compare. In His Word we can find the wisdom that we need for all of our life's decisions.

God's Word can be communicated to people in different forms to convey God's power for saving his people. God's Word can be conveyed to Christians through the inspired words of the Bible and through other Christian writings. God's Word is conveyed to Christians through the sacraments to offer forgiveness of sins. Christian conversation and sermons can allow for God's Word to work in the lives of believers. New technologies are also allowing God's Word to be proclaimed in different ways through video, music, quick messages, and other forms of media.

Studying God's Word can be done through its various forms to provide guidance for Christians. It will not usually work to randomly open the Bible to a chapter and hope that it will relate to the question that a person has. A couple years ago I led a Bible study on the temptations of Jesus in Luke 4:1-13. (If you have access to a Bible read through the verses in Luke 4) The preparation that I did for the Bible study can illustrate how Christians can study God's Word.

I have a study Bible that contains useful helps for understanding the Scriptures. Related Bible verses are listed in the margins next to verses. One of the verses that related to Luke 4:13 was Hebrews 4:15. *For we do not have a high priest who is unable to sympathize with our weaknesses, but we have one who has been tempted in every way, just as we are—yet was without sin.* Jesus experienced temptation just like we do so he knows what we are going through when we are tempted. Our weakness turns into strength when we rely on Christ.

There is also a concordance at the back of my study Bible where I can look up a specific word and see where in the Bible the word is used. I used the concordance to look up the word "temptation". There were eight verses listed. There was one that I felt spoke especially to how Christians can rely on God when they face temptation. *No temptation has seized you except what is common to man. And God is faithful; he will not let you be tempted beyond what you can bear. 1 Corinthians 10:13* When Christians are facing temptation it is empowering to know that God will provide them strength to resist the temptation.

When reading through the verses in Luke chapter 4 I also remembered another verse that was related to temptation. *If we confess our sins, he is faithful and just and will forgive us our sins and purify us from all unrighteousness. 1 John 1:9* Only Jesus lived a perfect life. If Christians are unable to resist temptation and fall into sin, they can be assured that God will forgive them when they confess their failure to follow His will. God delights to forgive and is always ready to restore His people.

Another useful resource when seeking guidance from Scripture is the Internet. I went to a search engine and typed in, "Bible verses on temptation". Many of the same verses that I had already looked at were on the web pages in the search results, but it is still a useful tool. There are also online concordances that can be used to search specific words in the Bible. Multiple versions of the Bible can be searched at the same time to provide different perspectives on a verse.

The Internet can be used to read others stories of how God communicates to them through His Word. There are also many resources for devotions or Bible studies. I went to a search engine and typed in, "ways to resist temptation." I was able to compile the following points on temptation. Each point is supported by Bible verses.

(1) Recognize temptation for what it is and that it's intent is to lead humans into sin. Read James 1:14

(2) Run away from temptation. Read 1 Corinthians 10:13 and 1 Timothy 6:11.

(3) Resist temptation with the Word. Read Hebrews 4:12 and 2 Corinthians 10:4-5.

(4) Repent when you fail. Read James 1:15 and 1 John 1:9.

(5) Refocus your thoughts with praise and worship. Read Psalm 147.[2]

When leading the Bible study I was able to discuss with other Christians what they thought about temptation. Asking other Christians for advice is one way God imparts His wisdom to us. Christian friends may know helpful Bible verses that they can share. Trusted Christian friends will hopefully also provide advice that reminds us of God's love.

Every time people have to make a decision they do not have to use a concordance, search the Internet, read related Bible verses, or discuss the decision with other Christians. However, if people are struggling with knowing what God would want them to do it is important to try to use as many resources as possible. This can help them to see what God would want them to do.

Out of His great love for us God sent His Son as an example for how we can live our lives. *In the past God spoke to our forefathers through the prophets at many times and in various ways, but in these last days he has spoken to us by his Son. Hebrews 1: 1,2a* Christians can rely on Christ's love for direction and protection.

Protection Through God's Word

The love of Christ involves Him always being there for us and never leaving us. The parable of the lost sheep is an example of this. The shepherd does not want to lose even one sheep so he searches for it until he finds it. Then he rejoices greatly at finding the lost sheep. In the time of Jesus, shepherds kept their sheep in pens with an opening on one end. In many cases there was no gate. You would think that the sheep would just wander out in the middle of night. However, the good shepherd is the gate. The shepherd would stay in the opening and keep the sheep safe from danger.

Similarly, Jesus keeps us safe from any dangers in life. This is a great message to proclaim. It is because of what Jesus has done and His love for us that we are able to love others and share the Gospel with them. Jesus loved us first by dying on the cross and wiping our sins away. He has secured a place for us in heaven and has a direction that he wants our lives to follow. The motivation to love others and share Christ's love comes from the Holy Spirit working in us.

Martin Luther's explanation of the first article of the Apostles' Creed states the blessings, which God gives us and the result of this in our daily lives.

> I believe that God has made me and all creatures;
> that He has given me my body
> and soul, eyes, ears, and all my members, my reason
> and all my senses, and still
> takes care of them. He also gives me clothing and
> shoes, food and drink, house
> and home, wife and children, land, animals, and all I
> have. He richly and daily
> provides me with all that I need to support this body
> and life. He defends me

against all danger and guards and protects me from all evil. All this He does only
out of fatherly, divine goodness and mercy, without any merit or worthiness in me. For all this it is my duty to thank and praise, serve and obey Him. This is most certainly true.[3]

These are the many blessings that God gives us for which we thank, praise, serve, and obey him.

But God does not just provide us with physical blessings for this life; through His Son's death and resurrection, He provides even greater spiritual blessings. As these blessings are conveyed to us through the Gospel message we are overwhelmed when we discover they are given to us freely. This good news of the Gospel is nothing that I can earn or win. It is a free gift from a gracious God.

This does not assume that life will be easy for the believer in Christ but God has promised to be there with us. *For surely, O Lord, you bless the righteous; you surround them with your favor as with a shield. Psalm 5:12* Christians can persevere in all situations knowing that God has promised life, hope, and a future. Christian singer Jeremy Camp has a song *There Will be a Day* with great lyrics about our journey in life.

> *I know the journey seems so long*
> *You feel you're walking on your own*
> *But there has never been a step*
> *Where you've walked out all alone*
>
> *Troubled soul don't lose your heart*
> *Cause joy and peace he brings*
> *And the beauty that's in store*
> *Outweighs the hurt of life's sting* [4]

Christians know what their final destination will be, and with that blessed assurance can freely live life for God.

Anyone who has used a GPS or directions from the Internet knows that they are not always accurate. They even have a disclaimer that the person should use common sense when following directions. If you are supposed to turn left but there is a fence, some cows, and a pond in the way it is probably not the best idea to follow the directions. In unfamiliar areas many streets have similar names and signs can be hard to see, making it even more likely for one to get lost.

In life if we try to find our way without God's direction we can become lost or confused. However, meditating on God's Word will allow Christians to see the path God wants them to follow. Christians can trust God's advice. He will provide accurate and wise direction for our lives. *Listen to advice and accept instruction, and in the end you will be wise. Many are the plans in a man's heart, but it is the Lord's purpose that prevails. Proverbs 19:20-21*

God promises us that if we believe and trust in His directions for life then we will reach our destination. *Trust in the Lord with all your heart and lean not on your own understanding; in all your ways acknowledge him, and he will make your paths straight. Proverbs 3:5-6* When my parents dog Lucky is the happiest is when someone who cares for him is guiding him. Lucky does not just have to rely on himself. Christians can rely on God for understanding and direction.

They know they are loved and blessed to have a God who cares for them and wants the best for their direction in life.

Chapter 3: The Word in My Pocket

All Scripture is God breathed and is useful for teaching, rebuking, correcting and training in righteousness, so that the servant of God may be thoroughly equipped for every good work.
2 Timothy 3:16-17

There is nothing wrong with men possessing riches. The wrong comes when riches possess men.
Billy Graham

It seems obvious now, but a couple of years ago I realized that God still has a lot to teach me about how to live as a child of God and how to show His gracious love to others. When I carry God's Word with me during the day and take time to meditate on it, then I become much more aware of the needs of others and become less focused on myself. There are plenty of people in physical, spiritual, or mental pain in the world; which can be eased with God's love and Christians generously serving others. If God's Word is in our hearts and mind than no matter what our possessions are we have a richness that far surpasses any understanding.

There is a picture, which is seen a lot, of a person holding their pockets inside out to indicate that they are poor or have nothing to offer. The empty pockets pictures are usually accompanied by someone whose face seems sad or ashamed. It does not seem like a desirable quality to have empty pockets. Americans are constantly inundated on television, radio, billboards, and the Internet with advertisements that tell us of the things we need to be happy. Advertisements are plastered everywhere. In some places now they even have advertisements on televisions in restrooms. It seems like there is no refuge from the barrage of messages. Try to make it through a day without seeing or hearing an advertisement where someone is trying to influence you to buy something. It will be a tough task unless one decides to hibernate for the day.

In choosing a career people can be influenced in a number of different ways as well. Different factors are important to help people decide what they think will make them happy. People's interests and talents can provide guidance for the career they will pursue. Job availability and pay are also items that people consider. For some, life is a contest of how much money they can make and how big a house they can have. They derive their happiness based on amassing possessions and wealth, but there is a more fulfilling way.

In the movie *The Bucket List*,[1] Jack Nicholson plays the part of a billionaire who could buy anything that he ever wanted. He is diagnosed with cancer and starts to search for the source of true happiness. After being befriended by Morgan Freeman, a character who also has cancer, he realizes that money and possessions are not the source of happiness. The movie does not have a blatant religious message but still points out a common theme of the folly of selfishness.

When you live your life for Christ, there is no doubt about where happiness can come from. Jesus has loved us so much that he died for us and promises to never leave us. *Hebrews 13:5 Keep your lives free from the love of money and be content with what you have, because God has said "Never will I leave you; never will I forsake you."* It can be easy to get caught up in the love of money. When things are going well people feel in control and that they can do anything for themselves. That is why Jesus said that it will be hard for a rich person to enter heaven. It will be easier for a camel to go through the eye of a needle. If we stop focusing solely on our needs, it is easier to become aware of the needs of others.

God's Word in my Pocket, Heart, and Mind

The main idea for writing this book came from God speaking to me through His Word when I was in a hospital in Vail in 2009. Since my major surgery in 2008 I had been trying hard to listen to my body and get more rest when needed. I was on different medication for my Crohn's disease that was more effective but stronger. A side effect of this medicine was that my immune system was weakened making me more prone to infections. I had switched schools where I was teaching at in the summer of 2009. I was now at a smaller charter school with fewer students that I would teach in a given day. Having grown up going to smaller Lutheran schools it felt like a better fit for me and definitely lessened my stress-load.

My school had a Friday off towards the middle of March and I had planned a trip to visit my younger brother who worked in Vail, Colorado. My older brother and his fiancé were coming as well. We were planning on going skiing for the weekend and I was excited for another chance at the mountains. I had been skiing there before, two years earlier, when I was just learning to ski. The scenery and mountains were breathtaking; at least when I was not falling and tumbling down the slopes. Even though I was a beginning skier and took some hard tumbles it was amazing to marvel at the beauty of God's creation. I had been skiing a couple times since then and was more confident in my ability as I prepared for the second trip.

Four days before we were to leave I began to get a fever and felt a bump forming in my lower back. Having learned from my previous experience not to wait till it gets worse; I went to the doctor and was prescribed some antibiotics. The day of the flight to Vail, I was still feeling kind of sick but felt that the medicine would help to turn it around. Having anticipated the trip, I did not want to miss going. The flight left around six in the morning. We flew into Denver and then had a little less than a two hour drive to Vail. Either the travel made me feel worse or the antibiotics were not working when we arrived at my brother's place I was not feeling well.

Later in the day when we went to rent skis for the next day, I knew that I should get in to see a doctor. I ended up in the emergency room and the doctor told me that I had a cyst that needed to be cut open and drained. Knowing that I was planning on flying home on Monday, the doctor decided not to take me to the operating room but to do the procedure with me awake. I was given painkillers and the procedure went well. I felt relief knowing that I would feel better. I was able to be released Sunday night so that I could fly back home on Monday.

Throughout the weekend I had time to think and reflect. It was an extremely disappointing weekend because it ended up going much differently than I had planned. I was grateful for the skills of the doctors and nurses who took care of me and that I had God as my constant companion. I had been in prayer during the weekend and was grateful for my faith in God. *The grass withers and the flowers fall, but the word of our God stands forever. Isaiah 40:8* While my earthly body will fail and wear down over time, it is comforting to know that God's Word and His love lasts forever.

Communication and relationships are a two way street though. I wanted to take more time to listen to what God had to say to me in response to my prayers. *Therefore, my dear friends, as you have always obeyed — not only in my presence, but now much more in my absence — continue to work out your salvation with fear and trembling, for it is God who works in you to will and to act according to his good purpose. Philippians 2:12-13*

In these two verses Paul is extolling the Christians in Philippi to not take their faith for granted. Paul is not saying that Christians need to earn grace and eternal life by works. He is emphasizing the importance of spiritual growth and development. The Christian life can be an ongoing process of becoming more like Christ in response to God's grace.

I had read the Bible during the weekend and started to think that there was a lot more that God had to teach me. Like many young adults I needed to realize that my relationship with God should not be taken for granted. I knew that by being in His Word daily I could accomplish this but wanted a way to make sure that I could do this and not lose focus.

The desire to learn more and grow in my relationship with God made me wish that I had a reservoir of Bible verses of comfort and wisdom to share with other people. The day before my Dad had double bypass heart surgery, several years ago, it took me awhile to find some good verses to read to him. I wanted to have some Bible verses memorized in my heart and mind that I could share with others. Many times due to the busyness of life when I hear a good Bible verse in church or discussion with others it does not stay with me for as long as I would like.

The idea came to me in the hospital in Colorado that when I would hear a Bible verse that would speak to me or one that I thought would be good to memorize, I would write it down. *For everything that was written in the past was written to teach us, so that through endurance and the encouragement of the Scriptures we might have hope. Romans 15:4* I started with a sheet of paper that I could fold up and put in my pocket that contained Bible verses that had special meaning to me. When I have free time or have to wait, I take out my sheet of Bible verses from my pocket and read through it. I take time to pray and reflect on what God is trying to teach me.

I have been carrying a sheet of Bible verses for a month at a time. During the month I write on my sheet of paper other chapters and verse numbers of passages that I encounter during my month. I then type those verses up and use these for my next month of Bible verses in my pocket. This has been a great way to stay in the Word and help me to think of others.

Meditating on God's Word

Repetition aids memory. Picking the number of Bible verses to put on your sheet and the length of time you carry it around will vary with the individual. If God is teaching you a lot from one Bible verse, it might stay on your sheet for a long time. You could also add your prayer list to the back of the sheet and use the time to pray for the needs and requests of those on your mind.

Having Bible verses in your pocket can allow for meditation on the Word of God. *But his delight is in the law of the Lord, and on his law he meditates day and night. Psalm 1:2 Do not let this Book of the Law depart from your mouth; meditate on it day and night, so that you may be careful to do everything written in it. Then you will be prosperous and successful. Joshua 1:8.* In the Old Testament times many people could not read or write. They needed to meditate on Scripture out loud and through conversation. This way they would not forget God's Word that had been shared with them. Meditating on Scripture can be a daily blessing and help you listen to God's wisdom and guidance for your life.

One way to meditate on a Bible verse is to pray first for the Holy Spirit's guidance. Then actually read the passage out loud several times. Think about how your life and personal needs relate to the passage and try to paraphrase the passage in your own words. Think about how this passage conveys God's judgment on your sin and also how the passage conveys God's gospel message. Think about what God wants me to know here, what would God like me to be, and what does God want me to do. Finally you can pray to God using the words of the passage and your thoughts to communicate to God.

Perspective from God's Word

Having Bible verses in my pocket allows me to receive wisdom from God in my life decisions. In 2010 I was living with two of my friends in a house that one of them owned while going to school for a doctorate in education. My friend that owned the house agreed to let another person and their dog move in for two months because they needed a place to stay.

I knew the person who was going to be moving in, but was angry that my friend had not even talked to me about the other person moving in beforehand. At the time I was feeling stressed with the workload of graduate school and was not looking forward to the extra stress of living with a new person and a dog. I knew it was my friend's decision to make but I at least wanted to let him understand my point of view.

The next morning I woke up still not feeling good about the situation. I knew that reading God's Word could provide me with guidance. I read through the Bible verses in my pocket and instantly felt at peace with the situation after reading the following two verses. *Do everything without complaining or arguing, so that you may become blameless and pure, children of God without fault in a crooked and depraved generation, in which you shine like stars in the universe. Philippians 2:14-15 I am not saying this because I am in need, for I have learned to be content whatever the circumstances. I know what it is to be in need, and I know what it is to have plenty. I have learned the secret of being content in any and every situation, whether well fed or hungry, whether living in plenty or in want. I can do everything through him who gives me strength. Philippians 4:11-13*

I realized that I had been foolish for being angry. I should have been happy that my friend was willing to open his house to someone that needed a place to stay. I was no longer angry but encouraged by his act of kindness. I knew that living with another person and a dog would be an adjustment. However, it was not really much to deal with compared to what other people in the world have to deal with on a daily basis. It is easy to take for granted basic comforts and conveniences that most Americans have.

It made think of how God really has blessed me. There are so many things that I have to be thankful for. I started to make a list of everything in my life that I can thank God for. In about five minutes I had listed close to 100 different things. Some of the items on my list were family, clothes, running water, computer, freedom of speech, not having to live in fear, plants, education, God's love, golf clubs, and snow. In the busyness of life it is easy to get in a routine of focusing on our own needs. When people take time to daily thank God for everything they have been given, it can help them to be content in any situation.

Witnessing through the Word

Keeping the Bible verses with you can also lead to opportunities to witness. They serve as an easy conversation starter. For example, someone might ask what are you reading. I guarantee you will find the verses useful and will have opportunities when it feels appropriate to share or discuss a certain Bible passage from your sheet with a friend, family member, or stranger. A couple years ago my brother had shoulder surgery. I talked to him before the surgery and found a couple verses on my sheet that I thought were appropriate to share with him. *The Lord is good, a refuge in times of trouble. He cares for those who trust in him. Nahum 1:7 Come to me, all you who are weary and burdened, and I will give you rest. Matthew 11: 28*

Sharing Jesus with others is not always the easiest thing to do. Corrie Ten Boom experienced things in her life that no one would want to experience but her faith in God only was strengthened through her trials. During World War II Corrie and her family used their home to hide Jews from the Nazis. The Germans eventually found out about what the Ten Boom family was doing and arrested the whole family. Corrie's dad died ten days after being in prison. While one of Corrie's sisters, brother, and nephew were released Corrie and her sister Betsie were sent on to concentration camps.

While they were held in captivity they did not lose their hope and faith in God's promises and love. *So if the Son sets you free, you will be free indeed. John 8:36.* These words of Jesus let Christians know that they are no longer held captive by sin. God's gospel truth allows Christians to know that they are a part of God's family. Christians can look forward to a glorious reunion in heaven.

Betsie talked to Corrie about what they would do when they were released. "The most important part of our task will be to tell everyone who will listen that Jesus is the only answer to the problems that are disturbing the hearts of men and of nations...We can tell from experience that His light is more powerful than the deepest darkness." Corrie was released ten days later due to a clerical error. Unfortunately, Betsie died three days after her conversation with Corrie.

After Corrie was released she devoted her life to being a world wide witness for Christ. In her book *Amazing Love* she describes her experiences of sharing the Gospel with people in different situations. One conversation she has is with a college student.

Ten Boom asks the college student a question, "what are you doing to bring the Gospel to your fellow students?" The student responds, "I feel very guilty this morning. I see myself suddenly as very much like the fireman who goes around straightening pictures while the house burns."[2] This is an extremely thought provoking statement about what our daily lives consist of. Am I simply going through the motions in a day and doing actions that serve my own purpose? Am I ignoring God's purpose for my life?

The world today is on fire in the sense that there are wars, people suffering, people in need of help, and many people are in need of the good news of Christ. There are people that are dying without God as their Lord and Savior. It is easy to take for granted how wealthy we are in the United States and how many freedoms we have. Fifty-three percent of the world lives on less then 2 U.S. dollars per day. If people have a bank account they are wealthier than 70 percent of the world. Thirteen percent of people in the world are hungry or malnourished.[3] There are many people who would benefit for help with daily needs but more importantly would benefit from knowing the love of Christ.

The United States is in need as well and other countries are sending missionaries to the United States. Sharing the Gospel does not just need to happen in other countries, but in our country, state, city, community, home, and with our family and friends. It can be a tough question to wrestle with but an important one to consider; is what I am doing in my daily life just straightening pictures in a burning house?

Christians do not have to go to another country to witness to others. There are many opportunities to witness to others that God places in our lives. When people get into a routine of daily living they often fail to notice these witnessing opportunities.

The social networking site Facebook can be a useful tool for such witnessing opportunities. Homepages on Facebook list birthdays and special events in people's lives. Recently I saw an event that gave me an idea for a quick way to witness to others using social media. The event was entitled, "Witness Workshop". The event served as a reminder to me that God desires me to share his Gospel message with others in my life and that social media is an outlet for this. It gave me the idea to do a daily post on Twitter for what God was teaching me through a Bible verse. Posts on twitter, or tweets as they called, are limited to 140 characters. People can share what God means to them and make an impact in the lives of others.

Some times witnessing to others involves just a few kind words. A man at my church was in charge of finding enough volunteers to ring the bells for the Salvation Army kettles that are in front of stores during the holidays. He jokingly called the group the ding-a-lings. Whenever anyone places money in the kettle he always responds with, "Thank you and I want you to know that Jesus loves you". One night he was volunteering and ringing in front of a store. His grandson was playing the trumpet as well to help out. A lady was standing and watching him for a while and he figured she was just listening to his grandson. After seeing several people place money in the kettle she approached and deposited some money in the kettle. The man from my church replied as usual, "Thank you and I want you to know that Jesus loves you." The lady replied, "I heard you say that to other people and I really wanted to hear you say that to me, thank you." The Word of God and the Gospel message are powerful. It is possible for any "ding-a-ling" to make a difference in another person's life because of the power of God.

God's Word is priceless

For any situation, life event or for any emotion there is wisdom that the Bible can impart. Taking the time to read the Bible everyday gives me insight into my life and relationships with others. Having Bible verses memorized helps my relationship with God and my relationships with others grow. Rob Bell in his book *Velvet Elvis* gives insight into how God can use Christians in the lives of others when we share His word. "Missions then is less about the transportation of God from one place to another and more about the identification of a God who is already there."[4] Sharing the Word of God with others can allow the Holy Spirit to work in their lives and give them wisdom for their lives. *So is my word that goes out from my mouth: It will not return to me empty but will accomplish what I desire and achieve the purpose for which I sent it. Isaiah 55:11*

Sometimes relying on ourselves can leave us coming up empty. Several years ago, in California a man tried to rob two banks and got away with nothing. The police did not catch him and he was nicknamed the empty pockets bandit. Sometimes desperation or what we see as a need for survival can lead people to do things that are dangerous and illegal. This is a fitting illustration of what happens when we rely solely on ourselves and go against what God would want for our lives. Our lives are empty without Jesus in control of them. The man's pockets were empty. If we trust in God through the tough times and the good times our pockets will never be empty.

For you know that it was not with perishable things such as silver or gold that you were redeemed from the empty way of life handed down to you from your forefathers, but with the precious blood of Christ, a lamb without blemish or defect. 1 Peter 1:18-19
God is our father, comforter, and provider. With God is great strength and riches in His grace. The free gift of eternal life in heaven is greater than any amount of money, cars or fame.

The book of Job describes how Job had lost everything. Job had all of his possessions and family taken away and was afflicted with painful sores. Still he did not lose his faith and said words that have been used in a number of places including in the work of Handel's Messiah. *I know that my Redeemer lives, and that in the end he will stand upon the earth. And after my skin has been destroyed, yet in my flesh I will see God; I myself will see him with my own eyes---I, and not another. How my heart yearns within me! Job 19: 25*

This is an amazing confession of faith. Job knew where his strength came from and who to rely on. He fixed his eyes not on earthly possessions but on his eternal life in heaven. Job knew that everything belongs to God and with this attitude one can approach life with hope. *The earth is the Lord's, and everything in it, the world and all who live in it. Psalm 24:1*

I heard someone say once that the true measure of a person is not the size of their strength but the size of their surrender. When we surrender our lives to God we realize that in our weakness we have strength because our Father in heaven can do awesome things. Even if our possessions are few and our pockets are empty we know that the **riches of God's Word can fill any empty pocket** or void and provide **hope** and **comfort** for all.

Chapter 4: Love from the Word

As the Father has loved me, so have I loved you. Now remain in my love. If you obey my commands, you will remain in my love, just as I have obeyed my Father's commands and remain in his love. I have told you this so that my joy may be in you and that your joy may be complete. My command is this: Love each other as I have loved you. Greater love has no one than this, to lay down one's life for one's friends.
John 15: 9-13

To love at all is to be vulnerable.
C.S. Lewis

The way to love someone is to lightly run your finger over that person's soul until you find a crack, and then gently pour your love into that crack.
Keith Miller

Human love may disappoint us and not live up to our expectations. However, God's love is more powerful than sin and can mend broken relationships. If we focus on God's self-sacrificing and perfect love for us; then we will never be disappointed in His love. It is only through actions and words grounded and motivated by God's love that Christians are able to show this similar self-sacrificing love to others.

Human love often involves some level of uncertainty. Relationships can take a lot of work to develop and can lead to two possibilities. Over time love can wane and people can begin to wonder if others really care about them. On the other hand people can develop long lasting loving relationships with family, friends, and significant others. Consider the example of marital love.

Since 1990 the trend has been that people in the U.S. are marrying later in life. Before 1990 there had been little in the way of sustained change of the marriage age for about hundred years. In 1890 the median marital age for men was 26.1 years and in 1990 the median age for men was exactly the same. In 1890 women married at a median age of 22 years and in 1980 the median age for women was exactly the same. Currently in the United States the marriage age for men is estimated to be 29 years and for women to be 27 years.[1]

What is the explanation for people in the U.S. waiting longer to get married in the past twenty or thirty years? One explanation could be that people's average life expectancy has been increasing. People are living longer so that they do not feel the need to get married at a younger age. However, life expectancy was increasing before 1980.[2] Another explanation could be that with the advance of technology and the Internet people are able to stay connected to more people. People have more options for a possible spouse than ever before. Many people do not want to settle for someone if they do not feel that they are completely in love. Evidence for this is that 88% of people in the U.S. ages 20-29 believe they have a soul mate waiting for them.[3] People are more willing to wait for this ideal soul mate than previous generations.

A third explanation for the increase in marital age focuses on the number of divorces in the United States. For the past ten years divorces in the United States have averaged around 850,000 to 950,000 a year.[4] Put another way one out of every two marriages in the U.S. fails. Marital vows are not taken as seriously in the current generation as they have been in the past.

Human relationships can and often do fail causing much pain. Our loving God is grieved by this. He offers through the sacrificial love of His Son a way to stem this painful trend. *And so we know and rely on the love God has for us. God is love. Whoever lives in love lives in God, and God in him.1 John 4:16* Relying on God's love and allowing God to work in a person's life can reverse the trend of failed relationships. He offers through His Son a love that is steadfast and trustworthy.

If God's love is not the model for human love it can lead to pain and disappointment. *We know that we have passed from death to life, because we love our brothers. Anyone who does not love remains in death. 1 John 3:14* Christians know that God's love in their life brings eternal life and hope. *Be imitators of God, therefore, as dearly loved children and live a life of love, just as Christ loved us and gave himself up for us as a fragrant offering and sacrifice to God. Ephesians 5:1-2.* Focusing on God's self-sacrificing love can allow Christians to use this as a model for their life. Keeping focused on God's trustworthy promise of perfect love for our life will never lead to disappointment.

There was a story on the front page of yahoo.com not too long ago about a couple that was about to marry. Usually when a couple marries one of them will change their last name. In this case it was not needed because both the first and last names of this couple were the same. It was a random introduction that started on Facebook that led to the couple's engagement. The female Kelly Hildebrandt, who lives in Florida, searched Facebook to see if anyone had her same name. There was only person who appeared in the search, male Kelly Hildebrandt who lived in Texas. She sent him a message and three weeks later he flew to Florida to meet her. After a whirlwind romance of eight months, they got married.[5] That is a story of how human love can be a powerful thing.

Love is something that people need and want to give to others. The word "love" can bring very different memories and emotions into the minds of people. What was the first thing that came into your mind when you read the word love? It may have brought good images and thoughts of loved ones. It could also bring negative thoughts and images because of times when we have been hurt or been betrayed by love. It takes a lot of courage for someone to express their love to another. If this love is mistreated or abused it can lead to deep feelings of hurt and pain. Because of this some people come to have a negative view on love.

God's Love for Creation

It is important to keep in mind where love came from and started. *Dear friends, let us love on another, for love comes from God. Everyone who loves has been born of God and knows God. Whoever does not love does not know God, because God is love.* 1 John 4:7-8 God first loved us by creating us in His image as it states in Genesis chapter one. God continued this love by sending His son to die for our sins so that we may have eternal life. *This is how we know what love is: Jesus Christ laid down his life for us. And we ought to lay down our lives for our brothers.* 1 John 3:16

God has great love and compassion for His creation and enjoys seeing when His work is accomplished through humans. *The Lord your God is with you, he is mighty to save. He will take great delight in you, he will quiet you with his love, he will rejoice over you with singing.* Zephaniah 3:17 God has made a beautiful world and people that are capable of amazing things that can give glory to God. Think about a time when you created or made something. It might have been something for work or school, a type of food, art, music, a poem, video, scrapbook, furniture, or anything else. It is a great feeling to create and an even better feeling to share your creation with others.

When I was growing up my mom thought it would be a good idea to have my brothers, sisters, and me surprise my dad with a meal when he came home from work. My siblings and I worked hard to make sure that the house was clean and that the food was perfect. My mom, my brothers, my sisters, and I all dressed up in our best clothes to serve the meal to my dad. When it was getting close for the time when my dad was to come home there was a lot of excitement and anticipation to see the surprise and happiness on my dad's face. The clock on the wall seemed to start to move slower. Soon it was 10 minutes past when my dad would usually get home, then 30, 50, and 75 minutes. This was before cell phones when a quick call could have cleared up any confusion. When my dad finally made it home the next day we were wondering what had happened. He had been at an overnight faculty retreat at a camp. He had told my mom about it, but she had forgotten. A week later we were able to prepare a meal again with the joy and satisfaction of seeing the happiness and appreciation on his face. Similarly God gets joy and satisfaction when he sees His creatures rejoice over His creation.

It can be a much different feeling if people work for a long time on something and it is ignored or they are told that it is no good. That rejection can be devastating and immobilizing. When we as humans belittle and mock others, in a way, we are telling God that what He has made is no good. *With the tongue we praise our Lord and Father, and with it we curse men, who have been made in God's likeness. James 3:9* When humans fight with each other and cause each other pain it goes against what God had meant for His creation. God is the creator of every person in this world and God loves each and every one of us.

On the cross Jesus showed how much He cares for His creation by paying the ultimate price for our sins. In so doing he freed us from the lies of the world that tell us that we are no good. *But now, this is what the Lord says--- he who created you, O Jacob, he who formed you, O Israel: "Fear not, for I have redeemed you; I have summoned you by name, you are mine. Isaiah 43:1* God calls each one of us by name, for He has redeemed us by sending His Son to pay the price for our sins. God's love for His creation has made each person unique and with special gifts. God does not desert His creation but continues to shower His love on it.

God's Love in my Life

The story of how my parents became engaged is a true love story. This was before the days of social networking sites and online dating. My mom's sister and her husband were the matchmakers for my parents. They knew my dad, who was a pastor in Nebraska at the time, and thought that he might be a good match for my mom who was teaching for a year in Australia. My dad and mom started to write letters back and forth, exchange photos, and even audiotapes were sent across the Pacific. The small town Nebraska postman even began to surmise that the preacher was in love. There was an attraction between them. My mom came back from Australia and agreed to meet my dad for the first time at her parent's farm. After having just spent one day with my mom, my dad was convinced that she was the one. He proposed to her that night and she said, "Yes". My parents have now been married thirty-seven years.

They have relied on God's love to support them in the good times and get them through the tough times. *Though one may be overpowered, two can defend themselves. A cord of three strands is not quickly broken. Ecclesiastes 4:12* This passage illustrates that God can be the third party to strengthen a marriage.

The love that my parents received from God they passed on to my two brothers, two sisters, and me. During my high school years there was a specific incident that came to mind for me that demonstrates this. When I was seventeen I was in a car accident, where thankfully no one was hurt, and my parents showed me that they still loved and trusted me. Since we did not have a lot of extra money growing up my parents always wanted to make sure that my siblings and I were safe drivers. There were only certain times that we were allowed to borrow the car to drive. This particular night was three days after my seventeenth birthday and my parents had agreed to let me drive to a friend's house. However, I was not supposed to drive anywhere else.

When I arrived at my friend's house, we decided to go and see a movie. Everyone else came up for excuses as to why they did not want to drive and, though I knew that I had promised not to drive anywhere else, I agreed to drive to the movie theater. It was a theater that I had not been to before and assumed that someone else knew the way there. It turned out that between the four of us in the car we were not sure how to get to the movie theater.

In the confusion that followed, I ended up driving though a stop sign and was hit by another car directly on the right side of my car. The car I was driving started to spin and crashed through a stop sign, a concrete bench, and a small pine tree. While the accident was happening I remember a feeling of protection over my body. It might have been the centrifugal force that kept me from moving or a guardian angel but either way I knew that God was with me and protecting me. The car I was driving was totaled but miraculously no one in either car was hurt.

It was a tough phone call that I had to make to let my parents know what happened. They listened to me as I told them about the car accident and they were relieved to know that no one was hurt. They were definitely disappointed, but knew that people are more important than possessions. I agreed to help pay for the repairs and apologized for having let them down. The next day as we were leaving the house my dad handed me the keys to my parents other car and said that I should drive. It was a sign that my parents still trusted and loved me even though I had made a huge mistake.

Sometimes our sins in life can weigh us down and cause us to feel that we are disappointing God. We feel that God could not possibly love us because of all of the bad things that we have done. However, God has promised that his love is unending and that all of our sins are forgiven. *As far as the east is from the west, so far has he removed our transgressions from us. Psalm 103:12* When we sin God does not leave us, but still wants to comfort and help us in our problems. *Though your sins are like scarlet, they shall be white as snow; though they are red as crimson, they shall be like wool. Isaiah 1:18*

When my parents forgave me for wrecking their car and disobeying them it did not compel me to want to do worse things but the opposite. Since I was shown love it compelled me to show love back by doing my best to obey my parents. The same is true for God's love in our lives. *As a father has compassion on his children, so the Lord has compassion on those who fear him. Psalm 103:13* Since God has forgiven us, it compels Christians to turn from our sinful ways and try our best to live a life for God. There is a song by Billy James Foote called, "You are My King", that tells of our response to God's love.

> *Amazing Love, how can it be? That you my King would die for me? Amazing Love, I know it's true; It's my joy to honor You. In all I do, I honor You.*[6]

One of my favorite verses in the Bible explains what God would have us do, confident in his unchanging love for us. *He has showed you, O man, what is good. And what does the Lord require of you? To act justly and to love mercy and to walk humbly with your God. Micah 6:8* Acting justly, loving mercy, and walking humbly with your God have a lot to do with our relationships with others in our life.

God's Love Will not Disappoint

Not everyone in life has a great relationship with his or her parents, which can make the image of God as a loving

Father difficult to comprehend. Children who grow up with negative relationships with their parents can have a more difficult time in life. In 1999 researchers carefully studied the lives of 17 school shooters and found three main themes. Every shooter was white, middle-class, and from a home in which the father was either absent, distant, or not involved.[7] Similarly, doctors from John Hopkins who did thirty years of research found that children's closeness to their parents contributed to them being less likely to develop certain health problems.[8]

Christian author Josh McDowell has talked about how God's love was able to work in his life despite a difficult childhood through the friendship of Christian friends. McDowell was sexually abused between the ages of 6 to 13 by a man that was hired to help on his parent's farm. On top of that McDowell's father was an alcoholic and would beat his wife. It was not until McDowell went to college that he was exposed to God's love. He met a group of Christians that showed God's love to others and he knew that he wanted more than anything else to experience a similar loving relationship.

McDowell states the importance of Christians' building relationships with non-Christians and taking the time to demonstrate through words and actions what God's love is all about. "People are desperate for truth that is grasped, grounded, and communicated in the context of relationships."[9] Christians need to take the time to build relationships with non-believers. Through God's Word non-believers can come to know God's grace and have a relationship with God as their loving father.

The Power of Love from God's Word

There is a story that a teacher told me to show the impact of love on the lives of humans. There was a king that wanted to know what language babies would speak if they were not spoken to at all after they were born. The babies were fed and changed but were not talked to or held much. They kept them all in a room together. The babies cried a lot and sadly ended up dying. The tragedy of this story reveals the fact that even though the babies' basic needs were met, they were missing the vital ingredient of love. Our bodies and souls are wired to give and receive love from others. *A new command I give you: Love one another. As I have loved you, so you must love one another. John 13:34* God did not create us to live in isolation, but to have fulfilling relationships with others. Because God has shown love to us, then we can love others.

My experiences in life and my years of teaching have demonstrated to me that people often need love the most when the world would say they deserve it the least. Mother Teresa knew the importance of love in her work with others.

> The greatest disease is not TB or leprosy; it is being unwanted, unloved, and uncared for. We can cure physical diseases with medicine, but the only cure for loneliness, despair and hopelessness is love. There are many in the world who are dying for a piece of bread, but there are many more dying for a little love.

During my first year of teaching I encountered some students that were receiving bad grades and were often a discipline problem. I remember talking to another teacher for advice. He told me that teachers often want their bad students to change their ways but teachers also must remember that we might need to change what we are doing as well. This caused me to think about what I could do differently. The students that I had the most difficulty with were students that I spent the least time talking to outside of class. I made it a point to seek these students out and do my best to show that I cared for them. It was not always a quick turn around but I could notice a difference. They caused fewer problems in class and appeared to be trying harder.

This lesson has stayed with me in my other classes that I have taught. I do my best to try to build a good classroom community at the beginning of the year. I show all of my students that I want them to succeed and care about their lives. Once students realize that a teacher values them; it motivates them to work harder. When they have been shown that they are important, they in turn respond with their best effort.

Some students are more difficult than others as they may not be used to being in a caring and supportive environment. They may require extra patience and more time. We can probably all think of someone that at times can drive us crazy with their behavior. However we can listen to God's wisdom for how we can treat others. *But the wisdom that comes from heaven is first of all pure; then peace loving, considerate, submissive, full of mercy, and good fruit, impartial and sincere. Peacemakers who sow in peace raise a harvest of righteousness. James 3:17-18* As God has forgiven us so many times then we can in response love and forgive others.

It is easier to forgive and show love to a friend or family member than it is to an enemy. But in Jesus time on earth he showed the example of how we should love all. *You have heard that it was said, Love you neighbor and hate your enemies. But I tell you: Love your enemies and pray for those who persecute you. Matthew 5: 43-44* Jesus often spent time with tax collectors and outcasts of society. Jesus spent time with these people while others would not want to even be associated with them. When Jesus looked at the poor, downtrodden, and neglected of society he did not see their shortcomings. Instead he looked at them as children of God.

There is an English proverb that goes, "faults are thick where love is thin." Showing God's love to someone that constantly annoys or hurts us is not always something that we think of doing. The power to do this comes from God and can have a huge impact.

A story that appeared in *Rolling Stone Magazine* in 2004 gives an example of forgiveness and love. Walt Everett[v] is a pastor of a church in Connecticut. It was a tough day for him when he learned of the death of his oldest son, twenty four year old Scott. Scott was shot and killed by a drug dealer and addict who lived in the same apartment building. For a full year Walt Everett's anger damaged his relationship with his wife and two remaining children and his work in his church.

About a year after his son was killed, Walt Everett attended the sentencing of his son's murderer, Mike Carlucci. Mike Carlucci had managed to get a plea deal to serve only five years in jail. Mike did not say much in the hearing but did say, "I'm sorry." Some of Walt Everett's friends did not hear much sincerity in the apology but there was something about it that changed the way Everett felt.

But now you must rid yourselves of all such things as these: anger, rage, malice, slander, and filthy language from your lips. Colossians 3:8 It can be difficult to let go of anger when someone has caused us pain. However, Christians know that as God's holy people we should clothe ourselves with compassion, kindness, humility, gentleness and patience. Through the power of God's love this is possible.

Everett decided to write a letter that entailed all of the pain that Mike had caused him and his family. At the close of the letter though, he wrote words that had been on his heart for the past couple of days, "I forgive you Mike." Mike wrote him back and expressed his deep regret for what he had done. The two continued to write letters back and forth.

After spending only thirty five months in jail Mike Carlucci was released from prison partly on pastor Walt Everett's backing that Mike be set free. What happened next is further proof of the power of God's love and forgiveness. "But almost four years later came the strangest twist of all:

With TV cameras whirring in the narrow vestry of a Methodist church in Bridgeport, Connecticut, Everett presided over the wedding of Mike and Sandie Carlucci."

Everett and Carlucci now speak at several schools and churches a year. Mike Carlucci recognizes that he himself is a changed man. "Asking God to forgive me opened me up," said Mike in an interview for the magazine. To Everett he said, "This is the man who taught me how to be human, gave me the opportunity to get my life back. What he did was unconditional love."[10]

Mike Carlucci is a Christian now and sees the world in a different view. Like all of us he is not perfect though and still has issues to work through. The unconditional love of Jesus was shown through Walt Everett to Mike Carlucci. This shows the power of God's love and forgiveness can change lives. *For God so loved the world that he gave his one and only Son, that **whoever** believes in him shall not perish but have eternal life. John 3:16* God wants us to show love to everyone, even those who we may see as enemies.

The Christian band Third day has a song called, "Born Again" that displays how when a person becomes a Christian, their view on love and life will change. God's love can reach and change anyone.

> *Today I found myself,*
> *After searching all these years,*
> *And the man that I saw,*
> *he wasn't at all who I thought he'd be,*
> *I was lost when you found me here,*
> *And I was broken beyond repair,*
> *Then you came along and you sang your song over me*

It feels like I'm born again
It feels like I'm living
For the very first time
For the very first time,
In my life

Make a promise to me now
Reassure my heart somehow
That the love that I feel is so much more real than
anything

I've a feeling in my soul
And I pray that I'm not wrong
That the life I have now, it is only the beginning[11]

God's blessed assurance is that life on earth is only the beginning and a far greater joy awaits in heaven.

Agape Love

When I was going into my freshmen year of high school, I went to a Lutheran basketball camp for a week with my younger brother. We stayed in cabins, played basketball outdoors, and experienced camp life in the woods. My camp counselor went by the name of Pickle and introduced me to the music of the Christian group Newsboys. The basketball was fun and we stayed up at night playing cards listening to Pickle's Newsboys CD's. During the week the counselors told us to be ready for the agape meal at the conclusion of the week. We tried to guess what that meant but none of the campers or I could guess the correct meaning. We had thought it was going to be some strange new food that we had not eaten before.

At the end of the week, all of the campers were told to gather outside of the dinning hall. We were escorted in by our camp counselors to the dinning hall. It had been decorated as if it were a fancy restaurant. Throughout the night the camp counselors waited on us as we ate and did their best to make sure we were happy with the meal. The main course we ate was spaghetti. We still did not completely understand what the agape meal meant. We thought maybe it was just a way to cook spaghetti like al dente.

After we ate, we came to understand the point of the night. The camp counselors explained that agape is a Greek word for love. It is the pure kind of self-sacrificing love that Jesus showed with his death on the cross. It does not judge but is unconditional love. *But God demonstrates his own love for us in this: While we were still sinners, Christ died for us. Romans 5:8* This is the unchanging love of Jesus. Christ did not die for our sins because of the great things that we have done. While we were still undeserving sinners Christ died for us out of love.

When we realize just how much God has forgiven us of and the depth of His love it can cause Christians to love God and others even more. *"Two men owed money to a certain moneylender. One owed him five hundred denarii, and the other fifty. Neither of them had the money to pay him back, so he canceled the debts of both. Now which one of them will love him more?" Simon replied, "I suppose the one who had the bigger debt canceled." "You have judged correctly," Jesus said. Luke 7:41-43*

In Jesus time on earth a denarius was a coin worth about a day's wage. When you think of the sins in your life, do you see yourself as the person who had fifty denarii forgiven or the person who had five hundred denarii forgiven? I know if I really take an honest look at my sins and myself I realize that I am the person who has five hundred denarii forgiven and more.

Realizing that by myself I am just a sinful person who is capable of nothing good can help me to rely on God. *The Lord is close to the brokenhearted and saves those who are crushed in spirit. Psalm 34:18* If you feel that you are a pretty good person and only need God during certain times of your life, you are keeping God at a distance. When we come to God recognizing our sinful nature and unworthiness than grace can abound in our whole life. *Have mercy on me, O God, according to your unfailing love; according to your great compassion blot out my transgressions. Psalm 51:1* These were the words of David after the prophet Nathan rebuked him for committing adultery with Bathsheba. David had to repent and ask God for forgiveness. David had strayed from God and knew that he had to rely on God's grace and mercy to restore him.

It is only through God's love that Christians are holy people capable of doing great work for God. This is the love that brightens Christians' spirits in good times and lightens their load in difficult times. This perfect agape love of Christ then compels us to show this love to others.

In 1 Corinthians Paul explains this love in greater detail. *Love is patient, love is kind. It does not envy, it does not boast, it is not proud. It is not rude, it is not self-seeking, it is not easily angered, it keeps no record of wrongs. Love does not delight in evil but rejoices with the truth. It always protects, always trusts, always hopes, always perseveres. 1 Corinthians 13: 4-7* This sounds like a lot for one person's love to live up to. But that is the beauty of it. Only Jesus, both true God and true man, could demonstrate this love for us.

There is a saying that I have heard, that the true measure of a person is how they treat someone who can do them no good. As sinful humans there is nothing that we had to offer God. *He saved us, not because of righteous things we had done, but because of his mercy. He saved us through the washing of rebirth and renewal by the Holy Spirit whom he poured out on us generously through Jesus Christ our Savior. Titus 3:5-6* It was out of his self-sacrificing love that he sent His Son to die for us that we might have eternal life in heaven.

If we base our love for others by looking at human love, it will always come up short. People may have had a disappointing relationship with their parents, friends, siblings, or significant other. If they look to the cross and focus on the awe-inspiring love that Jesus has shown for them, then they will never be disappointed by His love.

Chapter 5: Life in the Word

The thief comes only to steal and kill and destroy; I have come that they may have life, and have it to the full.
John 10:10

"God will cause you to grow. His purpose when He leads you into His Word is never just to inform or entertain. He means to change you."
Milton Rudnick from his book *Journey into Prayer.*[1]

The meaning of life and how life started has been debated and talked about for centuries. Sadly many people search their whole lives to find the meaning of it all and are never satisfied with what they find. Throughout time people have commented on life. The Greek philosopher Socrates said "An unexamined life is not worth living." His view on life focuses on reflection and thought. Abraham Lincoln took a different view on life, "And in the end, it's not the years in your life that count. It's the life in your years." The message is what we accomplish and do in our time is the most important. Poet Robert Frost, took a bland view on life, "In three words I can sum up everything I've learned about life. It goes on." Musician John Lennon, of the Beatles felt that, "Life is what happens while you're busy making other plans." The best-laid plans might not always work out the way they are envisioned. The thirty-ninth president of the U.S. Jimmy Carter offered yet a different view on how life worked; "We should live our lives as though Christ were coming this afternoon." Which of the many different views on life will bring the most fulfillment? Christians need not doubt or wonder. The meaning of life is clearly laid out in Jesus's plan and purpose for them.

Growing up with two brothers and two sisters I heard and said more times than my parents probably wanted to hear that something is not fair. It might be that my older brother and sisters got to stay up later than I did or they got more cookies. In school, as well, a common complaint of students to a teacher is that their discipline is not fair. A good life lesson that I learned early on, was that life is not fair. In some ways it is good that life is not fair. The Christian band, Newsboys, has a song that talks about the true fairness of life.

> *when we don't get what we deserve*
> *that's a real good thing*
> *when we get what we don't deserve*
> *that's a real good thing*
>
> *born to sin*
> *and then get caught*
> *all our good deeds*
> *don't mean squat*[2]

The Bible is clear on the consequences of sin. *For all have sinned and fall short of the glory of God. Romans 3:23 The wages of sin is death. Romans 6:23* As sinners we deserve death. There is nothing that we can do by ourselves to correct the situation. *And everything that does not come from faith is sin Romans 14:23* All of the good deeds and a life lived well will not change the scenario. However, it is a fortunate thing when we get what we don't deserve. The second part of Romans 6:23 reveals the great exchange. *But the gift of God is eternal life in Christ Jesus our Lord.* Jesus takes our sins and in exchange we get His righteousness and the gift of eternal life.

There are many ways to destruction and death. However, there is only one way to heaven by relying on God's grace for our life. *Enter through the narrow gate. For wide is the gate and broad is the road that leads to destruction, and many enter through it. But small is the gate and narrow the road that leads to life, and only a few find it. Matthew 7:13-14* The road to eternal life is through Jesus and his love. **We do not deserve eternal life. It is only through what Jesus has done for us that it is possible.**

Eternal life is God's free gift to us. *I am the way and the truth and the life. No one comes to the Father except through me. John 14: 6* Christians have assurance that, because of what Jesus has done, in heaven all of our needs will be met. *Never again will they hunger; never again will they thirst. The sun will not beat upon them, nor any scorching heat. For the Lamb at the center of the throne will be their shepherd; he will lead them to springs of living water. And God will wipe away every tear from their eyes. Revelations 7:16-17.* In Christ there is life. There need be no fear of death. *Before long, the world will not see me anymore, but you will see me. Because I live, you also will live. John 14:19* Because of this Christians can rejoice. *So with you: Now is your time of grief, but I will see you again and you will rejoice, and no one will take away your joy. John 16:22*

God's Law for our Relationships

Eternal life in heaven definitely beats the alternative of hell, but what about Christians' life on earth? I have heard some people say that the life Christians live is not fun and that there are too many rules to follow. It might be easy for an unbeliever to view Christianity as a set of rules. Some people's view on life is to have as much fun as possible and not sweat the details. Comedian Rodney Dangerfield joked that people should "Always look out for Number One and be careful not to step in Number Two." If we only look out for ourselves, it will be easy to fall or step into the lies that the devil would have us believe.

God's rules or law is often said to have three uses in the life of a Christian; a curb, a guide and a mirror. Thinking of their common uses in everyday life gives insight on how the law can be viewed. A curb keeps a car from going off of the road. If people were to drive over the curb they could injure themselves or others. In the same way the purpose of God's law is to protect people from being hurt. A guide often provides direction. God's law provides direction for how Christians should live their lives. A mirror shows a person what they look like. In the same way God's law shows Christians their sins. All people are sinners and cannot live up to God's law.

As I was growing up, my parents had rules for me about my bedtime, how much candy I could eat, when I could drive the car, how I should treat others, and other rules that I did not always appreciate when I was young. As

I grew older I came to realize my parents had rules because they loved me and wanted to take care of me. Similarly, in any teaching position or management position of others if there are rules and regulations but no sign of caring or concern it will make for a hostile community. *My son, do not despise the Lord's discipline and do not resent His rebuke, because the Lord disciplines those He loves, as a father the son He delights in. Proverbs 3:11-12* However, in the context of a loving relationship with God it is easy to see the need for rules and guidelines.

God has given us rules not that we should feel burdened or weighed down but so that people do not get hurt. *Blessed is the man who does not walk in the counsel of the wicked or stand in the way of sinners or sit in the seat of mockers. But his delight is in the law of the Lord, and on his law he meditates day and night. Psalm1: 1-2* Meditating on God's law and relying on the Holy Spirit's guidance can allow Christians to be blessed in their relationships with others. Following the advice of the wicked or mocking others will only lead to people getting hurt.

The eighth commandment is to not give false testimony against your neighbor. Telling lies or gossiping about someone will only end up hurting others. *Reckless words pierce like a sword, but the tongue of the wise brings healing. Proverbs 12:18* Hateful words can cause a situation to become much worse. On the other hand some times it only takes a few well-chosen words to help fix a tense situation.

When I was in 8th and 9th grade I worked as a caddy at a golf course and experienced first-hand the importance of using well chosen words to help calm anger. Anyone who has played golf knows that it can be a frustrating game. Mark Twain once said that, "golf is a good walk spoiled." At times I had some tough golfers to deal with when their golf game was not going well. On one occasion I caddied for a golfer that was new to the golf course. On one of the holes on the front nine there was a small pond down the fairway on the left side. I did not mention the pond to him and of course he hit his tee shot towards the left. As we walked up to find the ball it was nowhere in sight. The man saw the pond and became angry that I did not mention it was there because his ball had probably landed in the water. I could have responded back that if he hit his drive straight it would be easier to find his ball or talked bad about him to the other caddies. However, I just decided to say the reason that I failed to mention the pond. I told the man that people do not usually drive the ball this far off of the tee on this hole. The man's anger went away instantly. He calmly said he would just drop a new ball, hit from here, and that next time I should let him know of any potential water on the course.

God's law is all about relationships. The first three of the Ten Commandments are about our relationship with God and the last seven are about our relationships with others. God desires that we have life and have it to the full in all our relationships.

What the World Offers

If people follow the advice of the wicked their lives will be much different. John 10:10 shows what following the wicked will result in. *The thief comes only to steal and kill and destroy.* The world can sometimes convey this as a view on life; that it is tough, and then you die. The message is that life is something that you survive and just try to make it through. This is a negative view on life that misses completely what life in Christ can be like.

The newest Rocky movie has a scene where Rocky is talking to his son about life. Rocky tries to keep him from making excuses.

> The world ain't all sunshine and rainbows. It's a very mean and nasty place and I don't care how tough you are it will beat you to your knees and keep you there permanently if you let it. You, me, or nobody is gonna hit as hard as life..... Now if you know what you're worth then go out and get what you're worth.[3]

Life at times can seem like it is one struggle after another that can be mentally, physically, and spiritually exhausting. A person feels exhausted but then another problem or set back happens. Actor Robert Strauss has a quote that can be used to describe what the struggle can feel like. "It's a little like wrestling a gorilla. You don't quit when you're tired, you quit when the gorilla's tired." Life will continue to happen. It is important to persevere.

Rocky goes on to explain to his son that life is not about the quantity of your problems but the quality of how you overcome the problems. Where the quote leaves off comes back to the question of what is the meaning of life and secondly where does our self worth come from? Is it based on our self-confidence or possessions? What can help people make it through their problems in life?

Christians know that by focusing on what Jesus offers their life will have meaning. Jesus offers comfort and rest from the trials of life. In the second half of John 10:10 Jesus says, *I have come that they may have life and have it to the full.* What does a full life in Jesus look like?

What Christ Offers

If we look at the opposite of what the thief comes for, there is a picture of what life in Christ is. *The thief comes only to steal and kill and destroy.* The flip side of this is blessings, life, and being built up with Christ as our foundation. Life in Christ does not involve having the joy or fun stolen from Christians but instead involves receiving innumerable blessings. Isaiah mentions some of these blessings. *For this is what the Lord says: "I will extend peace to her like a river. As a mother comforts her child, so will I comfort you. When you see this, your heart will rejoice." Isaiah 66:12a,13a,14a*

Similarly, Francine Rivers in her powerful book *Redeeming Love* has a note at the end of it about how her life has been blessed by trusting in God as her Savior.

> I used to believe the purpose in life is to find happiness. I don't believe that anymore. I believe we are all given gifts from our Father, and that our purpose is to offer them to Him. He knows how He wants us to use them. I used to struggle to find happiness. I used to work hard to attain it. By the world's standards, I was successful. But it was all

meaningless vanity. Now, I have joy. I have everything I ever wanted or dreamed of having: a love that is so precious I can find no words to describe it. I haven't achieved this through my own efforts. I certainly have done nothing worthy to earn it or even deserve it. I have received it as a free gift from the Lord, the everlasting God. It is the same gift He offers you, every minute, every hour, every day of your life.[4]

Many people spend their lives struggling to find happiness. Eric Weiner traveled around the world to different countries to learn what brought happiness to various people. In his interesting book *The Geography of Bliss* he details his travels and what he discovered about the pursuit of happiness. In Switzerland he found that people visit zoos more than sporting events, have a connection to nature, and like that their country is clean and organized. In Thimphu, the capital city of Bhutan, people are happy even without much in the way of technology. The city has no stoplights and did not have television until 1999. Weiner went to Iceland because studies have shown that people are happier in colder climates. In colder climates people have to rely on each other more to survive. In Qatar the ruling family gives everyone free healthcare, education, and there are no taxes. Weiner visited Moldova because it has been rated as the unhappiest country in the world. He found that people did not trust anyone because they think their government is corrupt.

Some times people feel that if they could just move to a different area they would be a lot happier. However, the book can be summed up in five words: paradise is a moving target.[5] If people look to places, possessions, and others to make them happy they will continue to think that something better is always out there to pursue. Whereas Christians know that real bliss comes from the trust and love that God offers.

Because of this should Christians always be happy? Jesus in His time on earth had a range of emotions. The Bible describes more than 20 different emotions that Jesus felt including anguish, anger, affection, compassion, distress, grief, gladness, joy, love, peace, sadness, sympathy, and weary. Christians may not always be happy, but they can have an inner sense of security, hope, and confidence in God's love for them.

This can lead to inner joy even while believers experience a range of emotions. *Be joyful always. 1 Thessalonians 5:16.* A Christian's sense of security and hope does not rely on a sunny day or possessions. It can be constant because of what Christ has done for us and His love for us. *Jesus Christ is the same yesterday and today and forever. Hebrews 13: 8 I have loved you with an everlasting love. Jeremiah 31:b* Reliance on our own feelings can betray us, because feelings fluctuate. However, God's promises to us do not.

Christ Offers Life

The thief comes to kill while Jesus came to give believers life. No other New Testament book uses the word, **life,** more than John. It is found thirty-six times in John while the next closest New Testament book uses it seventeen times. *In him was life, and that life was the light of men. John 1:4* Christ is the light in our lives, the reason for our hope and joy. The contrast between light and darkness is often used in art and movies. Darkness is often associated with evil and a need for caution. In the light nothing is hidden.

For with you is the fountain of life; in your light we see light. Psalm 36: 9. Jesus offers us a life of goodness and security. Psalm 23 is used a lot to talk about what trust in God brings. *He restores my soul. He guides me in paths of righteousness for his name's sake. Even though I walk through the valley of the shadow of death, I will fear no evil, for you are with me; your rod and your staff, they comfort me. Psalm 23:3-4* Jesus walking with you in life brings answered prayers, comfort, and guidance. The well-known poem *Footprints in the Sand* tells the true joy of life in the Lord. Our Lord carries us during our saddest and most troubling times.

Christ as our Strong Foundation

Finally the thief comes to destroy while Christ wants to build us up as members of the body of Christ for the fullness of life. Watching the Olympics is one of my favorite things to watch on television. Athletes train their whole lives for a single race or contest that in some cases can be half over by the time you finish reading this sentence. Each country takes pride in what their athletes can accomplish. One event that I like to watch is weightlifting. There are two lifts the weightlifters attempt. The athletes have three attempts at a snatch and three attempts for the clean and jerk. The power, focus and explosion of these athletes are evident in each attempt. Weightlifters must be in the right position and right mindset to avoid serious injury. If they do not have a strong core and strong legs they could be injured by the weight.

Pyrros Dimas[v] is a famous weightlifter from Greece who captivated his country with his strength and power during the Olympics. In the 1992, 1996, and 2000 Olympics he won the gold medal. He was nicknamed "The Greek Lion of Himara", his town of birth, and "Midas" for his strength. No athlete had ever won four consecutive gold medals in weightlifting. The 2004 Olympics were held in Dimas's home country of Greece and the stage was set for history. Going into the 2004 Olympics he was recovering from knee surgery and a hurt wrist. The odds were stacked against him but the home crowd was behind him.

On his last attempt of the weightlifting competition he put four hundred fifty-seven pounds on the bar. If he was successful with this Herculean lift he would earn the gold medal. The crowd fell silent as he prepared for the lift. He completed the clean portion of the lift, which involved bringing the weight to shoulder height. Dimas needed to just complete the jerk portion by pushing four hundred fifty-seven pounds over his head and holding it there until the judges agree that it is controlled. He exploded the weight up but it was too heavy, as he was unable to get it over his head, and the weight fell to the floor.

It would have been hard to tell though that he had failed at the attempt. As the home crowd gave a fifteen minute standing ovation, Pyrros Dimas took off his shoes and left them to signal his retirement. This five foot six inch, one hundred eighty-seven pound man had inspired the whole country. Pyrros strong foundation of strength allowed him to still capture a fourth Olympic medal, the bronze, based on his previous lifts.[6] The strong foundation of a weightlifters body is vital for his or her success. How much more inspiring and trustworthy is God's strong foundation for us. Relying on Christ as our foundation allows Christians to have victory over death and the devil and fullness of life.

The clean and jerk lift is similar to what Christ does in the life of a Christian. Jesus has **cleaned** or washed away all of our sins. *As far as the east is from the west, so far has he removed our transgressions from us. Psalm 103:12* His death on the cross has **jerked** away the devil's power. Jesus our Messiah has conquered death and defeated the devil once and for all. Martin Luther's explanation of the second article of the apostle's creed explains it this way:

> I believe that Jesus Christ, true God, begotten of the Father from eternity, and also true man, born of the Virgin Mary, is my Lord. Who has redeemed me, a lost and condemned person, purchased and won me from all sins, from death, and from the power of the devil; not with gold or silver, but with His holy, precious blood and with His innocent suffering and death, that I may be His own and live under Him in His kingdom and serve Him in everlasting righteousness, innocence, and blessedness, just as He is risen from the dead, lives and reigns to all eternity. This is most certainly true.[7]

If Christians are struggling with something or feel that some negative influence has power over them; they can be confident in the fact that Christ can comfort and help in all of the problems and pain in life. We can rest in His unfailing love and the comfort of his wide open arms. There is no doubt about Christ's strong foundation. He will always lift us up. *Humble yourselves before the Lord, and he will **lift** you up. James 4:10* Christians are humble because they know the saving work is all God's. Jesus will never fail on his lift; the victory over death has been won. Christians know that they are victorious and always are winners by relying on Christ's strong foundation.

Jesus gives an example of what a strong foundation in Christ looks like. *He is like a man building a house, who dug down deep and laid the foundation on rock. When a flood came, the torrent struck that house but could not shake it, because it was well built. Luke 6:48.* When we rely on the Word of Jesus as our foundation, no matter how much the weight of the world seems to keep us from victory, we can handle the trials and tribulations of life and be sure that we will not fall. If we rely solely on ourselves or others we can be moved and our foundation will crumble.

Jesus time on earth involved troubles and rejection as well, but He overcame any obstacles for us. *The stone the builders rejected has become the capstone. Psalm 118:22* Jesus repeated these words in his life on earth a week before he died for our sins. He knew that he would be rejected, suffer humiliation, and be crucified. Jesus did it out of his love for us so that our sins may be forgiven.

Jesus desires for Christians to be blessed, have eternal life, and be built up by relying on his sure and trustworthy foundation. *In that day the Root of Jesse will stand as a banner for the peoples; the nations will rally to him, and his place of rest will be glorious. Isaiah 11:10* In the Old Testament times Christians were given the gift of eternal life by their trust in the coming Messiah. Isaiah prophesized about the coming Messiah about 700 years before Jesus' time on earth. *But in these last days he has spoken to us by his Son. Hebrews 1:2a* Jesus, who was a descendant of Jesse, came to redeem all people. Christians know that an eternity of glorifying God in heaven awaits because of Jesus sacrifice on the cross.

Think of how Christ has been the strong foundation in your life as you read or sing a few verses of one of my favorite hymns written by Henry F. Lyte, *Abide with Me* and the Bible verse from Luke on which the hymn was based. The meaning of life is not complicated. Abide with God and let Him rule your life. Henry F. Lyte died shortly after writing the hymn.[8] He died with the comfort of having lived a life with Christ as his constant companion and strong foundation; as well as the hope and sure promise of eternal life in heaven.

But they urged him strongly: Stay with us for it is nearly evening; the day is almost over. So he went in to stay with them. Luke 24:29

Abide with me; fast falls the eventide;
The darkness deepens; Lord with me abide.

When other helpers fail and comforts flee,
Help of the helpless, O abide with me.

I fear no foe, with Thee at hand to bless;
Ills have no weight, and tears no bitterness.
Where is death's sting? Where, grave, thy victory?
I triumph still, if Thou abide with me.

Hold Thou Thy cross before my closing eyes;
Shine through the gloom and point me to the skies.
Heaven's morning breaks, and earth's vain shadows flee;
In life, in death, O Lord, abide with me [9]

Chapter 6: Service through the Word

For even the Son of Man did not come to be served, but to serve, and to give his life as a ransom for many
Mark 10:45

If you cannot speak like angels, If you cannot preach like Paul,
You can tell the love of Jesus, You can say He died for all.
Hymn stanza: Hark! The Voice of Jesus Crying[1]

Jesus set the example for Christians to follow by being humble and serving others. Meditating on God's Word throughout the day can open believers' eyes to all of the opportunities there are to serve others. Christians can use the gifts that God has given them to serve others and trust in God's strength when He is calling them to do what seems too difficult. When Christ accomplishes great things through us, we should give Him praise. In all Christians do we are to give glory to God.

Many times when people have reached a milestone or have an important achievement, they have the opportunity to make a speech or say a few words. Graduations, award acceptances and retirements are often filled with accolades and thank yous. On the other hand some speeches involve pure self-love and a touting of one's accomplishments. Others are humble, knowing that God has blessed them with gifts, and acknowledging many others who helped along the way. When Martin Luther King Jr.

was awarded the Nobel Peace Prize in 1964, he took the time to thank those who were not receiving recognition but who have helped him and others along the way. "Men and women will know and children will be taught that we have a finer land, a better people, a more noble civilization - because these humble children of God were willing to suffer for righteousness' sake."[2]

Christians can be humble knowing that any good that they do comes from God. *Every good and perfect gift is from above. James 1:17a* Jesus performed many miracles in his time on earth. If ever a person deserved to boast about his accomplishments, that person would be Jesus. However, he was humble and let all praise go to God. *The one who sent me is with me; he has not left me alone, for I always do what pleases him. John 8: 29 I am not seeking glory for myself. John 8:50a This is to my Father's glory, that you bear much fruit, showing yourselves to be my disciples. John 15:8* Jesus lived a life of service based on God's love. *As the Father has loved me, so have I loved you. John 15:9a* Any good deeds that Christians do is in response to God's love and the Holy Spirit working within them.

Knowing that God first loved us, then we can share this love and serve others. Jesus stated clearly that service follows from having a life in Christ. *Whoever serves me must follow me; and where I am, my servant also will be. My Father will honor the one who serves me. John 12:26* God's redeeming love motivates and empowers us to share the Gospel message with others through lives of service.

Commitment to Service

Don Meyer[v] was the men's basketball coach at Northern State University in Aberdeen, South Dakota. In 2009 he set the record for most coaching victories in the NCAA. In 2010 he retired from coaching with a whopping 923 wins. The number of wins is not the amazing part of his story though. The ESPY's are an annual awards show the sports channel ESPN does to award excellence in sports. In 2009 he won the Jimmy V Perseverance ESPY Award. Jimmy V (Valvano) was a men's basketball coach who won the NCAA championship in 1983. He died in 1993 as a result of bone cancer. The Jimmy V foundation seeks to raise money to find a cure for cancer.

September 5th, 2008 changed Don Meyer's life forever. He was involved in a car crash after falling asleep and drifting head on into an oncoming semi. As the doctors at the hospital worked to save his life, they found cancer in his liver and small intestine. During his recovery in the hospital he had to have one of his legs amputated and endure a long road to rehabilitation. After being in the hospital for fifty-five days he was released. The following morning he was at the gym at 4:45 coaching his players.[3]

During his acceptance speech at the ESPY's on ESPN, Don Meyer explained the principles that he lives by and teaches his players. He commented that the "F" word is used too often in society today but that his basketball team uses "F" words too. Don Meyer said, "Our F words are faith, family and friends. Faith that God has a reason for sparing my life at this time so that I can try to serve others for a few more years." It is an amazing statement from a man who feels a true calling to serve and improve the lives of the young men that he coaches; not only in their basketball lives but also in their academic and spiritual lives as well.

Jesus Set the Example of Service

Jesus time on earth set the example for all on how to live and treat others. *I have set you an example that you should do as I have done for you. I tell you the truth, no servant is greater than his master, nor is a messenger greater than the one who sent him. Now that you know these things, you will be blessed if you do them. John 13: 16-17* Jesus had just washed His disciple's feet when he said these words. This job was usually reserved for the least important person. Here the all powerful Savior of the world had cleaned the dirty feet of His disciples. He washed away the dirt and the grime, as He would soon wash away all of their sins on the cross. It was an example of selfless sacrifice that Jesus wanted his disciples to follow. Again, because of what Jesus first did for us, it allows us to go and humbly serve others.

When I was twenty-one I had the opportunity to help lead the youth group from my church in a week long servant event in Montana. While we were there we did some painting and worked on houses on the Crow Indian Reservation. Every night we had some devotion time. The night before driving back to Minnesota the devotion time included a foot washing that our group did for each other. After a week of working outside in the heat and a limited amount of showers; the other two leaders and I washed the feet of each youth from our church individually and then prayed for them. Then as leaders we washed each others feet and prayed for each other. It was a moving and powerful experience.

Now, I personally do not like the idea of touching someone's dirty and smelly feet. However, the lesson is that when we are serving others sometimes we have to get our hands dirty and do things that are not always to our liking. Michael Card has a song called, "The Basin and the Towel", that describes how Jesus washing of the disciples' feet is a call for Christians to live a life of service to others. Following Jesus example we can do these things with joy and a spirit of humbleness knowing that Christ has made the ultimate sacrifice for us.

> *Their Savior Servant must show them how*
> *Through the will of the water*
> *And the tenderness of the towel.*
>
> *And the call is to community,*
> *The impoverished power that sets the soul free.*
> *In humility, to take the vow,*
> *That day after day we must take up the basin and the towel.*[4]

The disciples had been with Jesus practically every day for three years, yet there were times when they still did not understand why Jesus had come to earth. They had seen Jesus preach and teach many people, heal various diseases and ailments, drive out demons, feed five thousand people with just five loaves of bread and two fishes, change water into wine, and perform many other miracles. Still they were not clear on the purpose of His ministry. It was when the disciples looked to the cross, the empty tomb on Easter morning, and saw Jesus in the evening that they finally understood.

How many times are there in the life of a Christian when we as well just do not understand? We can focus on the cross, the empty tomb, and how Jesus lived his life on earth in service of others to provide guidance for our lives. Jesus came to serve and give His life as a ransom for many. Because of what Jesus has done, Christians can serve others.

Where to Serve

Where are there opportunities to serve others? Service to God and leading a life of service to others can be done among family, friends, coworkers, and in our community. Everyone has unique gifts and talents that they can use to serve others. *The body is a unit, though it is made up of many parts; and though all its parts are many, they form one body. So it is with Christ. 1 Corinthians 12:12* If we neglect a part of our human body, our body does not function as well. Similarly, when Christians do not use their gifts to serve others, the body of Christ or God's church does not function as well. Through service Christians can be gifts to others by sharing God's love with deeds to help and to heal.

Church is a great place to serve others. There are many different ministry areas where churches need volunteers. When people volunteer their time they will help further the mission of the church and at the same time get to know other church members. People can serve in their church with youth groups, Sunday school, planning committees, music ministries, ushers, finance committees, food preparation, fundraising, building upkeep, landscaping work, outreach ministries to the unchurched and immigrants, and many other areas. If people are unsure of where their talents lie they can listen to where God is leading them to serve and fill in where there are needs.

Non-profit organizations as well are great places to serve others. Many organizations depend on volunteers to accomplish their mission. Habitat for Humanity, Feed my Starving Children, homeless shelters, Meals on Wheels, Union Gospel Mission, and many other organizations are more than happy to have people serve.

Serving others can be done with short term and long-term missions as well. If people feel God is calling them to serve for a week, a month, half a year, or a couple years there are many opportunities for missions trips in the U.S. and around the world. The LCMS (Lutheran Church-Missouri Synod) has a listing of service opportunities that can be searched by time length, region, country, or type of service at www.lcmsworldmission.org/service. Church bodies and other organizations can be contacted as well for more information about opportunities to serve.

I have been on a couple week-long mission trips. It is a great way to bless others with your time, talents, resources, and by sharing God's love. A surprise that I realized on my first mission trip was that the people that I served were a tremendous blessing to me, as well.

In Jamaica I was blessed by the enthusiastic desire for God's Word that the children displayed. When I was a student at Concordia University in St. Paul, Minnesota I was a part of the organization, The Concordia Mission Society, and went with a group to Kingston, Jamaica. We were able to go into the schools and share the good news of Christ through skits, songs, and conversations. The students' excitement to hear and talk about Jesus was overwhelming. They sang their hearts out to give praise to God and danced around the room. While the children had a great time, I think we should have planned our visit towards the end of the day. The teachers had a hard time settling down the students so that they could continue with their schoolwork. The childlike faith and exuberance of these students gave me a newfound appreciation for my relationship with God.

On another trip with the Concordia Mission Society I went with a group to Chihuahua, Mexico. In Mexico I was blessed by the generosity and kindness of a pastor and his family. The pastor of the church we were working with graciously provided housing and food for our entire group, close to twenty college students. The pastor and his family cooked amazing home cooked meals for us each day. We were able to help with construction of a new church, cleaning, and landscaping work. The pastor and his family were not rich but were willing to share what they had with us. Though they did not ask for anything, our group took up a collection to help pay for the food they provided and to further the ministry of their church. The amazing generosity of the pastor and his family helped me to learn to be more grateful for the many blessings I have in my life and to be more generous with what God has given me.

There are plenty of opportunities to minister to people right here in the U.S. as well. For example, young college students Mike Yankoski and Sam Purvis, took a phenomenal leap of faith in order to understand how they could minister to the homeless. For five months the two young men lived on the streets of six different American cities. They experienced extreme hunger pains, exhaustion, depression, and social rejection. They found that there is a great need for people to minister to the homeless. The young men sang Christian songs, played their guitars, and offered hope to people on the streets.

In San Diego they met a homeless man named Rings that invigorated their spirits. Rings had a tough life and described how knowing Jesus changed his life. "Been a trucker, a carnie, a door-to-door salesmen, a husband, a father. I've been in jail, been an addict, been a drunk. Now I follow Christ. All that I have is His. If He can save me, He can save anybody." "It's been a crazy road, that's for sure. But come-the road up ahead is always better than the road behind. Let's get started."[5] He still is homeless but has a new outlook on life. Whenever he is able to get money he cooks food for other homeless and shares the love of Jesus with them.

While church and other organizations are great places to serve, people can serve others in their everyday life as well. People can take the time to talk to others about their life and be willing to help others if they have questions or need assistance. Service could involve helping people move, picking up a person from the airport, cooking a meal for a friend, providing breakfast or treats for co-workers, or many other acts. When Christians are focused on the needs of others, then many opportunities of service will present themselves.

Shine God's Love Through Service

In all we do we are to give glory to God. People have many different gifts and abilities. Olympian, Eric Lidell whose life inspired the movie *Chariots of Fire,* said this about his gifts. "I believe God made me for a purpose, but he also made me fast, and when I run, I feel God's pleasure." Using our gifts to their maximum potential and giving credit to God can reveal the power of the glory of God to others.

My high school tried to instill the same idea in their students. The school's choice of mascot reflected this goal. Many people did not understand my high school's mascot. I went to a Lutheran high school, Concordia Academy, whose mascot was the Beacons. Often mascots are chosen to portray strength, power, create excitement, or to instill fear in an opponent. A Beacon at first glance does not seem to accomplish these goals. However, there is strength and power in the symbolism of a Beacon.

A Beacon is a guiding device such as a lighthouse. Lighthouses protect ships from getting too close to shore and also serve to provide direction for ships lost at sea. Christians, as well, can be beacons for the world. Through our service we can protect and provide direction for others. Sharing how our relationship with God provides meaning and direction for our lives can help others struggling to find direction in life. Christians can be beacons to light the path to heaven. *In the same way, let your light shine before men, that they may see your good deeds and praise your Father in heaven. Matthew 5:16* This Bible verse was painted on my high school gym wall. The teachers and staff tried to instill in the students that they could be beacons. In the classroom, in the community, in sports, or fine arts, the mission of Concordia Academy is to shine the good news of Christ to others. Humble service in the name of Jesus can brighten lives all over the world!

One example of the mission of Concordia Academy that relates to the lifelong impact of Lutheran education relates to how the football team ends every game. When things are going well it can be easy to praise God and serve others. However, when life is tough it is even more valuable to rely on God and give thanks for the strength that can be drawn from faith in God. Recently there was a news story of a football player that dropped an easy game winning touchdown. After the game the player blamed God for dropping the pass and expressed his anger that God would let this happen. When our focus is our own needs we lose sight of what God has done for us through His gracious saving love. In all we do and in all of life's events it is possible to give glory to God. I played football for Concordia Academy when I was in high school and after every game whether we won or lost our football team did the same thing. After shaking the other teams hand we would gather at midfield. Then as a team we would all sing the doxology.

Praise God, from Whom all blessings flow;
Praise Him, all creatures here below;
Praise Him above, ye heavenly host;
Praise Father, Son, and Holy Ghost.

Not everyone was a good singer. Not everyone was in a good mood if we had just lost a game or even sometimes if we had won the game. However, the message that was instilled in us was that no matter what happens in life, our focus can be on being a light in this world for others. Our whole reason for being is to give praise and glory to God. Life is not always easy and there are defeats and triumphs, but God never leaves us.

Rescue, sustain, and carry

During the course of a day there are opportunities to serve that we could never anticipate. Stephanie Carpluk never expected to need to be rescued at her job as a manager of a carwash in Massachusetts. On a slow February morning John O'Leary paid for his carwash and relaxed in his car as the car wash machine moved his car along the track. Stephanie walked behind John's car and was about to go into the office when she felt a tug at her neck. Her scarf was caught in one of the motorized shafts. Stephanie struggled to free herself but could not and blacked out from the pressure of the scarf tightening.

John had seen her go behind his car and when the soap cleared from his windshield he noticed that she was in trouble. John quickly jumped out of his car and went to where Stephanie was caught. He used a pocket knife that he had with him and managed to cut the scarf to free her. She was not moving though. He performed mouth to mouth resuscitation and managed to get her to breathe. Stephanie spent a couple days in the hospital but managed a full recovery. Stephanie was grateful and had a new outlook on life.[6] On her own she could have never freed herself no matter how hard she struggled. She needed someone to rescue her.

Similarly Christians know that on their own they would be dead to sin. People can feel like the weight of their sins and mistakes is strangling them. They feel they cannot breathe. Guilt for sins and feelings of inadequacy can make people feel that their situation is hopeless. Instead of wallowing in guilt, Christians can rejoice in God's gracious act of freeing us from sin and calling us to a new life in Him. Thanks be to God He sent his Son to die and rise again so that Christians might be rescued from the power of sin and the devil.

It is God's saving grace that gives Christians life. Christians know that God will sustain and carry them. This is not just when we are in old age but in all stages of our life.

Even to your old age and gray hairs I am he, I am he who will sustain you. I have made you and I will carry you; I will sustain you and I will rescue you. Isaiah 46:4 God sustains and carries Christians through his word, sacraments and through other Christians. Taking care of the needs of others by serving or helping them might allow the Holy Spirit to work in another's life.

For I was hungry and you gave me something to eat, I was thirsty and you gave me something to drink, I was a stranger and you invited me in, I needed clothes and you clothed me, I was sick and you looked after me, I was in prison and you came to visit me... The King will reply, I tell you truth, whatever you did for one of the least of these brothers of mine, you did for me. Matthew 25: 35-36,40 God works through people's acts of service. God's redeeming love can let us to know that He will carry us through life and has rescued us from the power of sin. Because of what He has done we can share his love by sustaining others with our service.

Strength for Service

Service to others does not always have to involve what we perceive as our strengths or talents. Sometimes what we perceive as weaknesses, God can use to demonstrate His strength in our lives. With the Holy Spirit working in the lives of believers nothing is impossible. In the Bible there are many occasions when God uses people with weaknesses to accomplish great things. The following was written by an unknown author and is adapted slightly.
Noah was a drunk

Moses stuttered & was a murderer.
Sarah was barren.
Leah was ugly.
Joseph was abused.
John Mark deserted Paul.
Timothy may have had ulcers.
Hosea's wife was a prostitute.
Amos' only training was in the school of fig-tree pruning.
Jacob was a liar.
David had an affair and was a murderer.
Solomon was too rich.
Abraham was too old.
Peter was afraid of death and denied Christ.
John was self-righteous.
Naomi was a widow.
Paul was a persecutor of the church.
Jonah ran from God's will.
Miriam was a gossip.
Gideon and Thomas both doubted.
Jeremiah was depressed and suicidal.
Elijah was burned out.
Martha was a worry-wart.
And Lazarus was dead!

In all we do we can rely on God and his strength. We do not need a great faith in God, but faith in a great God. The psalmist describes the greatness of our God. *Your ways, O God are holy. What god is so great as our God? You are the God who performs miracles; you display your power among the peoples. Psalm 77:13-14* In our strengths and weaknesses we can serve others and show the love of God to them.

In Joshua's final words to the Israelite people he summed up his desire for life. *But if serving the Lord seems undesirable to you, then choose for yourselves this day who you will serve.....But as for me and my household, we will serve the*

Lord. Joshua 24:15 Many people keep these words of Joshua posted in their homes as a reminder to serve others.

Bible verses can be a guide for our paths in life and how we can serve others. For a long time when I was going somewhere I had not been before I would usually put directions down on various scrap pieces of paper. Since I have now been carrying around Bible verses on a sheet of paper in my pocket I write directions to places on my sheet. On one side of my sheet I have directions to destinations. **On the other side of my sheet I have directions for how Christ would want me to live in the confidence of my eternal destination**.

When I am driving with directions to a location I know that I am never lost. I may drive by things and have to turn around but I am never lost. The same is true about having God's directions in my pocket and most of all in my heart for my life decisions. I may go by something that does not seem right or is something that I do not want to do. However, in the end, I learn that it was the right path to take.

When I was in eighth grade I did not like having to give speeches or talk in front of a group of people. I went to a small Lutheran school so my eighth grade class had only twenty-four students. About halfway through the school year the discussion came up one day about who was going to be valedictorian and salutatorian for the class. Grade point averages were shared and it became apparent that I was probably going to be valedictorian. It seemed great at first and I was proud of the hard work that I had done. That was until that I realized that I was going to have to give a speech at graduation.

I started to try to think about ways that I could try to avoid giving a speech. It would be an honor to be valedictorian but I decided that I could do without it. I made the decision that I would start missing questions on tests on purpose and not try as hard on my homework. I was hoping that I would be able to drop my grade point average to third in the class, because the salutatorian also had to give a short speech.

After a couple of weeks of this mindset I realized that it was not working. It seemed that I was being nudged by the Holy Spirit in a different direction. Not trying to do my best was against what I really believed in so I was never totally committed to my plan. I had been raised to know that God has given everyone gifts, which should be used to the best of their abilities. *So whether you eat or drink or whatever you do, do it all for the glory of God. 1 Corinthians 10:31*

In school the teachers even had a song that they would often have us sing to help us know that we should make the best use of our gifts from God. *Good, better, best. Never let it rest, till your good is your better and your better is your best.* When I trust in God and listen to his guidance then I know He will lead me to the right decisions. Giving a speech would be something that I could get through with God's help. I committed myself to finishing the rest of the school year with my best effort.

I ended up being valedictorian and now had the task of trying to decide what to say in my speech. In my first couple of drafts of the speech I decided to thank the teachers and talk about some memorable events that our class had experienced. It seemed like the speech was missing an important part though. The school where I went was East St. Paul Lutheran and I decided to try to use the letters ESPL for a theme for my speech. With a little help from my mom I found a good way to sum up my experience at the school. Every Student Praise the Lord. The focus of the school was not just on education, but on Christian education and how I could live my life as a child of God. The teachers, staff, and students showed that in all things there are opportunities to praise the Lord for His mighty power and great love. That is a great message to remember throughout the day; how can I praise God in what I am going to do today?

Though I was nervous the night of graduation, I was able to deliver my speech confidently. I knew then that my moment to be in front of others and be recognized had nothing to do with what I had accomplished, but had everything to do with giving glory to God for what He had accomplished. The next school year the administration decided to use Every Student Praise the Lord as the theme for the year. I had not wanted to give a speech and tried to avoid doing it. God had other plans, though.

There are many instances in the Bible where people try to avoid or hide from what God wants them to do. However, God is constantly seeking us out for His purpose.

Adam and Eve tried to hide from God when they realized that they had sinned in the garden of Eden, but God sought them out. Moses had no intention of leading the Israelites out of slavery but God came to him in the burning bush. God called Deborah to unite Israel. God called out to Samuel when he was a young boy. Jesus called the twelve disciples to drop everything and follow him. God came to Saul on the road to Damascus to call him to a new life in Christ. And God calls to each one of us today to live a life in the grips of His grace. *If anyone speaks, he should do it as one speaking the very words of God. If anyone serves, he should do it with the strength God provides, so that in all things God may be praised through Jesus Christ. To him be the glory and the power for ever and ever. Amen. 1 Peter 4:11* I pray that you have heard God's calling for a life lived in His love. God seeks us out, removes our sinfulness, and replaces it with holiness.

God can call Christians to serve in a variety of ways. Where in your life can you hear God calling you to service? Maybe you have had a feeling that you should bring encouragement to coworkers, go on a missions trip, work with a non-profit organization, serve with a ministry at church, volunteer your time, do yard work for a neighbor or friend, talk to others about your relationship with God, or many other things.

While working on this book I felt God calling me to work with a non-profit organization to benefit Lutheran education. I am extremely grateful for the quality Christ-centered education that I received. I believe that anyone who desires to send their children to Christian schools should be able to have that option available. However, I know that not everyone has the financial resources to attend Christian schools. It can be a great blessing for children to be in God's Word daily at Christian schools through religion classes, chapel, and conversations with teachers, staff, and other students. The foundations of staying in God's Word and discussing it on a daily basis for a believer's whole life can be developed through the schooling experiences of Christian education.

Sometimes God puts situations in your life that seem so obvious that you wonder why you did not see it sooner. My Dad is on the board of directors of the non-profit organization, the Lutheran Education Foundation of Minnesota (LEFM). When he was talking about the work of LEFM, it dawned on me that this is where God is calling me to serve. I joined the board of directors of LEFM and believe that the work of the organization has and can continue to make a powerful difference. The mission of LEFM is to provide financial assistance for low-income families that want to send their children to Lutheran schools. LEFM also provides resources to Lutheran schools so that they can continue to offer quality Christ-centered education.

Unfortunately the grade school that I went to, East St. Paul Lutheran, had to close several years ago. With tougher economic times, it is imperative now more than ever to support the work of Lutheran schools. The life long impact of the schooling experience that Lutheran schools provide cannot be underestimated. The staff and teachers at Lutheran schools are excellent, but they would be the first to tell you that it is the power of God's grace and love alone that makes the experience of Christian education powerful. Students are not just empowered to be successful in life, but they are empowered with the strength and confidence of knowing that God's wisdom will guide them through their lives. Students at Lutheran schools know that they can give glory and praise to God in all that they do.

The proceeds from this book are being donated to LEFM and to support families through Christian outreach in the communities surrounding urban Lutheran schools. My mom is the lead teacher for an ELL (English Language Learners) program[v] for Karen adults. The ELL program incorporates Bible stories and Christian songs with English acquisition. The Karen are a Christian ethnic group originally from Burma. They have been immigrating to the United States to escape persecution from the military government in Myanmar. The Karen families are eager to adjust to life in the United States and are appreciative of any assistance. With tough economic times there are many families in need of basic life necessities and God's love.

The hymn *Hark, the Voice of Jesus Calling* by Daniel March describes how Christians can be called to serve. When Christians hear God calling them to service in their life they can answer gladly, send me.

Hark, the voice of Jesus calling," Who will go and work today?
Fields are ripe and harvests waiting, Who will bear the sheaves
away?"
Long and loud the Master calls us, Rich reward He offers free;
Who will answer, gladly saying, "Here am I, send me, send
me"? [1]

God has a general destination for our lives to serve
Him and give Him glory in all that we do. By staying in
God's Word and meditating on it, our relationship with God
can grow along with our service to others. God wants us to
have life and have it to the full. May the following verses
stay with you as you live a life of service because of God's
sacrifice for you. *May the words of my mouth and the meditation*
of my heart be pleasing in your sight, O Lord, my Rock and my
Redeemer. Psalm 19:14

Your attitude should be the same as that of Christ Jesus: Who,
being in very nature God, did not consider equality with God
something to be grasped, but made himself nothing, taking the
very nature of a servant, being made in human likeness.
Philippians 2:5-7

Chapter 7: Staying in the Word

Those who belong to Christ Jesus have crucified the sinful nature with its passions and desires. Since we live by the Spirit, let us keep in step with the Spirit.
Galatians 5: 24-25

You have trusted Him as your dying Savior; now trust Him as your living Savior. Just as much as He came to deliver you from future punishment did He also come to deliver you from present bondage. Just as truly as he came to bear your stripes for you has He come to live your life for you.
Hannah Whitall Smith

A Christian's relationship with God can shape his or her life through staying in God's Word. God has created us all and desires to be in our whole life and not just part of our life. When Christians stay in God's Word, the Holy Spirit will work in their life so that they know God in a more meaningful personal way that will make their relationship with God become richer and stronger. When this happens Christians are shaped increasingly into His image.

People thrive on having fulfilling relationships. Whether it is with family, friends, co-workers, husbands, wives, boyfriends, or girlfriends; relationships with others allow people to express themselves and get feedback from others. Relationships offer support, encouragement, and an opportunity for fellowship and fun. There are times we may feel that we do not need others. The last words of H.G. Wells were "Go away. I'm all right." Whether we want to admit it or not the truth is that everyone needs relationships in their life. There are two old sayings that are debated as to which is true: out of sight and out of mind or absence makes the heart grow fonder. If you do not see someone or communicate with them for a day, week, month, or a year are you more likely to forget about them?

Studies have shown that both sayings are true. If we have a good relationship with someone in our life over shorter amounts of time absence makes the heart grow fonder; but over longer periods of time out of sight and out of mind becomes true. If we do not see someone or communicate with them they will slip from our mind.

The textbook for a class I took on social psychology stated that the best indicator of whether two people would start a relationship and keep it going is physical proximity or nearness.[1] If we do not see someone enough or communicate with them, we can take that relationship for granted and it will start to fade away. Communicating in our relationships and not taking them for granted are important if we want to continue to have meaningful relationships with our family, friends, and loved ones.

God desires for believers not to take for granted our relationship with Him as well. In order to continue to grow and learn in our relationship with God it is important to communicate with Him, by studying the Bible and prayer.

Then we can avoid the trap of "out of sight and out of mind."

Have you ever run into someone that you have not seen in a couple of years? At first it might be difficult to think of the person's name or even where you know them from. The ensuing conversation usually revolves around the basics of what each of you has been doing lately. Then you might not see the person for another couple of years.

With relatives or friends that live far away it might be a long time between face to face communications. Talking on the phone, email, or social networking sites might be ways to stay in touch, but out of sight will eventually lead to out of mind. I have found that with relatives and friends that I do not see often I am not good at remembering details about their lives. When maintaining relationships the important stuff is in the details.

While humans may have a hard time remembering, God never forgets about us. *The Lord remembers us and will bless us. Psalm 115:12a* It is amazing to think that the all powerful Lord and creator thinks about each one of us. He thought about us when He sent His son to die on the cross for our sins. And even if we have not talked to God in awhile, He still has us on his mind and knows about us. Jesus said that, *Indeed, the very hairs of your head are numbered. Don't be afraid; you are worth more than many sparrows. Luke 12:7* God does not forget about the birds of the air, the fish of the sea, or any of His creation. There is no need for fear because God will not forget us as well.

The mere fact that God thinks about and knows each one of us is humbling. God thought about us when He created us and continues to think of us our whole life. *For you created my inmost being; you knit me together in my mother's womb. Psalm 139:13* I want to think about Him as well because God is my joy, comforter, and redeemer.

The birth of a child is an amazing event. The beauty of God's creation is evident in each child. David described the beauty in this way. *I praise you because I am fearfully and wonderfully made; your works are wonderful. Psalm 139:14* Witnessing the birth of a child is not an event that is soon forgotten. Amy Singley and Steve Smith both have been present for the first few hours of a child's life. It just happens to be that they were present for each other's first hours of life. Amy and Steve were born on the same day, in the same hospital, and their mothers shared a hospital room. Their connection did not end there though.

Growing up their families both went to the same church, but they only knew of each other as sharing a birthday. That changed when they were 16. Steve asked Amy out on a date and after the second date Amy was pretty sure that he was the right guy for her. After a year of dating Steve wrote her a poem called destiny. It seems like their lives were destined to be together and in fact they got married after seven years of dating on June 12th, 2010.[2]

God was there for all of our births and has been with us our whole lives. Have there been times in your life when you took God for granted and only saw Him when you were at church? God desires for our relationship with Him to be a life long love. Christians want to make sure that their relationship with God does not become something that is important only during certain times in their life. When life gets busy people can become complacent with their relationship with God. It is important though, to keep God at the center of one's whole life.

The parable of the talents in Matthew 25: 14-30 gives an illustration of those who become complacent with God and do not use their gifts to help others. A master gave different amounts of money to three of his servants before leaving on a journey. The first two servants, who were given more than the last servant, took the money and doubled it. The last servant took his money and buried it in the ground.

The master returned and talked to his servants to see what they had done with the money. He was pleased with the first two. *"Well done, good and faithful servant! You have been faithful with a few things; I will put you in charge of many things. Come and share your master's happiness!" Matthew 25:21* These two servants had not taken for granted the gifts that the master had given them. Their relationship with the master grew and their blessings grew as well. They had used their gifts for good.

James describes what happens when believers exercise their relationship with God. *In the same way, faith by itself, if it is not accompanied by action, is dead. But someone will say, "You have faith; I have deeds." Show me your faith without*

deeds, and I will show you my faith by what I do. James 2: 17-18
Good deeds of service to others flow as a result of faith.

The third servant was afraid of the master and handed back the same amount of money that he had been given. The master replied, *"You wicked, lazy servant!....Take the talent from him and give it to the one who has ten talents. For everyone who has will be given more, and he will have an abundance." Matthew 25: 26, 28.* The third servant was thrown out into the darkness and was treated harshly by his master. The servant had done nothing with his gift. He was complacent with his gift and just gave back what he had been given. Because of this he was not invited to share in his master's happiness.

Fear or guilt is not the reason why Christians serve others. A story that highlights this involves a pastor who gave his congregation the wrong message. A pastor was leaving a fast food restaurant after finishing eating when he noticed a bell and a sign by the door. The sign underneath the bell read, "If your service was great ring the bell." The pastor instantly thought it would be a great idea to have a similar sign by the door at his church. He figured it would be a great way to tell if people had enjoyed the church service that week. The pastor went out and got a bell and installed a sign by the church exit that read, "If your service was great this week ring the bell." That week the pastor put extra effort into making sure that his sermon was going to be good.

When Sunday morning came the pastor preached with all of his gusto. At the conclusion of the church service he excitedly went to the back of the church to shake hands with the congregation as they exited. The pastor anticipated hearing the bell be rung as he was talking to people, but did not hear anything.

As he talked to the last person to leave, he thought that maybe the bell was broken. He went out by the church exit to inspect the bell. He found that it was working fine. There was a long time member still in the lobby. The pastor decided he would ask him why no one rang the bell.

The member shifted uncomfortably a little bit and responded, "well pastor you had such a good sermon that talked about how we should help others. I think most people felt guilty that they had not served others as much as they could this past week. If I had to rate my service to others, I would probably say that it was anything but great." The pastor had focused too much that week on worrying about what others thought about him. His message to his congregation was not clear and made them feel guilty that they had not served others.

Many people do not understand the true motivation for service. Some people view all religions as having similar ideas. The Dalai Lama said " Every religion emphasizes human improvement, love, respect for others, sharing other people's suffering." If this is the true, what is different about Christianity? While most other religions are works based

Christianity is faith based. Good works and service to others does not allow Christians to earn their way into heaven.

Christians' service towards others is not done to receive praise from others but to receive praise from our Heavenly Father. True service to others flows from the love that God shows to us. It is the Gospel message that empowers Christians to show this love to others.

The third servant in Jesus parable was not thinking that he might get thrown into the darkness or that he could share in his master's happiness. He was taking his relationship and gift for granted. It is important that we do not get in the habit of burying and not using the gifts God has given us. By meditating on Scripture and listening to what God has to say for our lives, our relationship with God can thrive.

Martin Luther in his explanation of the Ten Commandments starts each of them with "we should fear and love God." The third servant feared his master but because there was no love he did not use his gift. There is too much at risk to simply take our gifts and bury them in the ground. Christians know that God has promised whoever believes in God as their Savior will have eternal life. At the same time faith without works is dead. As a result of what God has done and His love for us then good works and service will flow from a believer with the Holy Spirit working inside of them.

Martin Luther described the Christian paradox of freedom as this, "A Christian is a perfectly free lord of all, subject to none. A Christian is a perfectly dutiful servant of all, subject to all." Christians have free will to make choices in their life. Eternal life is not anything that we have to earn. We just have to trust and believe in God as our Savior. At the same time Paul offers a caution. *So, if you think you are standing firm, be careful that you don't fall! 1 Corinthians 10:12* The natural response of faith in God is service towards others. Christians that take their faith for granted can be standing on a slippery slope. *But everyone who hears these words of mine and does not put them into practice is like a foolish man who built his house on sand. Matthew 7:26* The wise person hears God's Word and puts it into practice. The wise person has a strong foundation of faith that can preserve through the trials and tribulations of life.

Christians can study God's Word and rely on the guidance of the Holy Spirit to do God's will. *Do not conform any longer to the pattern of this world, but be transformed by the renewing of your mind. Then you will be able to test and approve what God's will is—his good, pleasing and perfect will. Romans 12:2* When people focus on God's will for their life they can withstand the lies and evil of the world. On the other hand when people take their relationship with God for granted it can lead to trouble.

How can we keep from taking our relationship with God for granted? Through daily Bible reading I came to realize I could keep my faith in my whole life rather than having my faith only as a part of my life. Meditating and reading the Bible can impart wisdom and allow God to communicate to believers. Communicating and having fellowship with other believers can also allow our relationship with God to grow.

However, a Christian's relationship with God always starts with God and what He does. Following are some ways to stay in the Word and fellowship with other believers so that a Christian's relationship with God remains centered in his or her whole life. The website wikihow.com has some ideas for how to keep a relationship fresh.[3] I have converted the ideas into a top ten list for keeping our relationship with God at the forefront of our life. Remember it is the Holy Spirit working in our lives that makes this possible.

Number ten: Take advantage of new technology. Talking to others about life is one way that God can communicate to us. Christians that are trusted friends or that have expertise in a certain area can be great to rely on for advice. When my parents needed advice in a variety of circumstances I noticed they would turn to different Christian friends for help. Staying in touch with these people through different modern means of technology like social networking sites, twitter, or texting can help.

There are a lot of resources on the Internet for a variety of topics. People need to be sure to be wise consumers of information but different blogs or websites can offer insight on life. Some churches have their sermons posted on the Internet. Watching videos of sermons can be a way to stay connected to God's Word if people cannot make it to church or just to get a different perspective on issues of faith.

Number nine: Hold hands, hug and give kisses often.
How can we hug God? This may seem difficult to do at first. However, it is possible to show affection to God by staying in communication with Him through prayer and studying the Bible. If a close friend wrote you a letter would you put it on the shelf and never look at it? God has a different letter for us everyday in His Word.

We may not be able to hold hands, hug and give kisses to God but we can show affection for His creation and our loved ones. God entrusted Adam in the beginning with naming and taking care of the creation. We too can show affection to God by thanking him for his amazing creation and making sure that it is not ruined. Passing along God's love to others in our life is another way to show affection to God. *Each of you should look not only to your own interests, but also to the interests of others. Philippians 2:4* Christians can treat others as God desires them to. Christians can thank and bring praise to God for the joy of having the unique personalities of others in their lives.

Number eight: Date often.
For relationships to thrive there needs to be time spent together. As I said earlier if we do not make time for a certain relationship it will start to fade. Christians can attend church regularly or be in fellowship with believers to spend time with God. This is a great way to give glory to God and be strengthened by Him as well.

The author of Hebrews states the importance of Christian fellowship for building up the church. *Let us not give up meeting together, as some are in the habit of doing, but let us encourage one another – and all the more as you see the Day approaching. Hebrews 10:25* Paul further states the importance of meeting together as a body of believers in Verses 12 to 27 in 1st Corinthians. The body of Christ is one, but has many parts that are all important for accomplishing God's purpose. *If one part suffers, every part suffers with it; if one part is honored, every part rejoices with it. 1 Corinthians 12:26*

Worshipping together with a community of believers also allows Christians to have assurance in God's promises of eternal life and forgiveness of sins through the sacraments. The basis of the Christian faith is that because of what Jesus did and offers, believers are saved. It is not because of the good works or great faith of an individual, and the sacraments reinforce this belief. Through baptism God gives the gift of eternal life and through the Lord's Supper believers receive assurance in the resurrection and the new life in Christ that he or she receives. In Communion, believers are continually reassured of what God has done and will continue to do for them. *For whenever you eat this bread and drink this cup, you proclaim the Lord's death until he comes. 1 Corinthians 11:26* Robert Kolb in his book, *The Christian Faith,* further describes the benefits of the Lord's Supper. "It builds anticipation and hope as we await the promise of the perfect celebration at God's heavenly table."[4]

The Lord's Supper bestows forgiveness and life, but it also links us with God and fellow believers as a family.

People can get excited about their relationship with God by experiencing strong fellowship with other believers. This can lead people to want to share their faith with others. When I was growing up I went to several LCMS national youth gatherings. Being a part of twenty to thirty thousand young people excited about their faith and praising God is a powerful experience. A Christian's faith in God's unending love is not based solely on emotion but it is a powerful feeling to fellowship with so many other Christians. The more time we share with God the more we will appreciate our relationship with Him.

Number seven: Write old fashioned love letters

Some people may think they are too old for a diary or a journal but it can be a great way to remember ideas and feelings. Journals are being used more often in many different subjects in schools as well. It is important to reflect on your thoughts and ideas in order to learn and grow. Metacognition is a powerful tool to have. Keeping a prayer journal can help keep your relationship with God fresh as well as your relationship with others.

Writing down my thoughts for this book has served as my journal. It has been great to see how God has been a constant companion through my life. I have also gathered greater insight in my relationship with Him as well.

Being able to come to God with all of your problems and joys is a remarkable thing. God has promised to answer our prayers. When people keep a journal about what God has taught them at various times in their life it may end up being useful for future problems or questions they may have. People may find themselves reading through their past thoughts and receiving insight for their present life.

Number six: Praise, praise and say thank you...and then give more praise.

One way that I learned to pray is the ACTS method. It stands for adoration, confession, thanksgiving, and supplication. People may find that they have nothing to pray about or are not sure what to say. The ACTS method is a good way for people to think through their life and find things to communicate to God. Adoration can be thought of as being in awe of God and simply listing out the reasons why He is incredible and inspiring. Confession would be talking about sins that a person is struggling with in his or her life. Then asking God for forgiveness and the strength to overcome them. Thanksgiving is a time to thank and praise God for all of the great blessings He has given in a person's life. Supplication involves humbly and earnestly presenting our requests to God, relying on His wisdom. We all have many blessings to be thankful for. God blesses us daily with many things that we can take for granted.

I heard Christian singer Bebo Norman tell a story that illustrates this point. Bebo was able to visit the children that he sponsors through the program Compassion International. The Compassion organization helps children in poverty around the world. The family that he visited talked about their blessings. The father said I have a hut, my family, a river to get water from, and a goat for food. There is nothing else that I need and I thank God everyday for his blessings.

Christians can take time to thank God for everything He daily provides. This can help us realize that God does provide for all things and we need not worry. *Look at the birds of the air; they do not sow or reap or store away in barns, and yet your heavenly Father feeds them. Are you not much more valuable than they? Who of you by worrying can add a single hour to his life? Matthew 6: 26-27* These words of Jesus extol Christians to focus on seeking God's kingdom and to not worry about earthly needs.

Number 5: Learn something "new" together.
God has countless things to teach us about life and ourselves. By experiencing new adventures people may find they will learn more about themselves and their relationship with God. By learning something new Christians may discover gifts or talents that God has given them that can be a blessing to others.

Music is one area where I like to learn new things. My parents are both good singers. When my siblings and I were young my parents made sure that we played instruments and sang in choir. When I was in college I was in choir for two years. I learned about my voice and how singing can be a powerful form of worship. Most of the choir members were better singers than I was so it was amazing for me to be a part of a gifted group of singers. *Come, let us sing for joy to the Lord; let us shout aloud to the Rock of our salvation. Psalm 95:1* Music is something I still enjoy. It can convey the power of a relationship and life rooted in God.

Learning new things can be a struggle at times as well. If a person is afraid of trying something new remember this saying; a ship is safe at port, but that is not what ships are made for. God has created us to learn our whole lives by using the gifts He has given us. God can teach us perseverance and show us His strength in our weaknesses. God's strength can be shown through others that God puts in our life. Relying on others for help allows them to share their gifts with us.

After I was in the hospital in 2008 my mom gave me the book *90 Minutes in Heaven* to read. The book is about Don Piper and his recovery from a horrific accident that involved a semi crushing the car he was driving. Don was pronounced dead at the scene of the accident but miraculously ended up surviving. He had a long recovery as his body sustained massive damage.

One part of the book stuck out to me as he described what he learned about allowing others to help him. "Just then I realized how badly I had missed the whole idea. I had failed them and myself. In trying to be strong for them, I had cheated them out of opportunities to strengthen me. Guilt overwhelmed me, because I could-at last- see their gifts to me."[5]

When I was in the hospital I did not want to be a burden to my friends and family. I usually would say that I did not need anything and that people did not have to stay long when they visited me. However, I was depriving them the opportunity to show their love to me and to allow myself to be strengthened at the same time. I needed to learn that a person cannot always be independent and that interdependence is a beautiful thing.

In all that we do we can worship and give glory to God. It might be learning to drive a car, starting a new job, fixing your car, raking leaves or any of life's tasks. It can be a blessing to others if we have a gift or talent that can be shared. Christians might not have ever thought about worshiping God with art, dance, music, construction, or fixing things but their relationship with God can grow as they share their gifts and abilities and learn new ones as well. *Praise the Lord. Praise the Lord, O my soul. I will praise the Lord all my life; I will sing praise to my God as long as I live. Psalm 146:1-2*

Number 4: Take a day trip to a new place neither of you have ever visited before.

Diversity and experiencing new cultures can help us appreciate God's people in new ways. It can also help us gain a different perspective on our relationship with God. When people visit a different country, state, city, or a different part of town they can see what the needs of others are and how to spread the Gospel message to them.

After Jesus resurrection Peter went to many different parts of the world telling the good news of Christ. *Peter replied, "Repent and be baptized, every one of you, in the name of*

Jesus Christ for the forgiveness of your sins. And you will receive the gift of the Holy Spirit. Acts 2:38. When Peter said these words he was addressing the crowd at Pentecost. The disciples had just declared the wonders of God to many different people in each person's own language. The message of the Gospel is not just for America or our friends but is for everyone. *This is good, and pleases God our Savior, who wants all men to be saved and to come to a knowledge of the truth. 1 Timothy 2:3*

When people experience new cultures and learn from them it can provide opportunities to build relationships where God's love can grow. Pastor Richard Crisco shares what it takes to reach others. "People really don't care how much you know until they know how much you care." Building relationships with others is not always easy but showing God's love to others can create opportunities to witness.

In visiting new places the beauty of God's creation is evident in the scenery and the landscape but also in the people as well. Actress and singer Pearl Bailey once said that "People see God every day, they just don't recognize him." God can be seen in a perfect sunrise, a relaxing conversation with an old friend, a kind smile, a hug from a family member, a warm bowl of soup, an act of kindness, encouraging words, and in many more daily occurrences.

Dan Ervin noticed this and started a website www.seegodtoday.com after witnessing the beauty of Mt. Rainier while on an airplane returning from a business trip.

After the mountain passed from view, he wrote down in his planner I saw God in Mt. Rainer today. In most of Dan's life he has found that he has been riddled by stress and anxiety. In the next couple of days after he had flown over Mt. Rainier he started to think, "I bet I see God every day and I am just too distracted to notice." His family started a routine that when they ate dinner together at night they would go around the table and take turns talking about where they had seen God today.[6] When we take time to appreciate and notice God's marvelous creation of nature, animals, and people it can be easy to see God in our daily lives.

Number 3: Strengthen your art of conversation.
People often have difficulty striking up conversations with random strangers or people that they would not usually talk to. However, the better we are at communicating the easier it will be to build relationships with our friends, family, loved ones, and even strangers. Christians can try having a conversation with just one person each day whom they would not usually communicate with. People will find that their communication skills will increase and the interaction could be a blessing to them and the other person.

God wants us to stay in communication with Him as well. God wants to hear our prayers and loves to listen to what we have to say. The whole day can be spent in communication with God. *Pray without ceasing. 1 Thessalonians 5:17* Communication is necessary for a relationship to grow and stay strong. Another method for knowing what to pray about uses the word "PRAY" (**Praise,**

Repent, Ask for others, and Your own needs). Jesus taught his disciples how to pray. In Luke chapter eleven, verses two to four, he gave them the Lord's Prayer.

God wants to hear our prayers and has promised to answer them. *Ask and it will be given to you; seek and you will find; knock and the door will be opened to you. John 11:9* Strengthen your art of conversation by praying to God throughout the day and watch God strengthen you throughout the day.

Number 2: Take care of yourself: mind, body, and spirit

How can Christians take care of their minds? Christians can take care of their minds by focusing on things that give glory to God. *Set your minds on things above, not on earthly things. Colossians 3:2* Our conversations with others, what we read, what we watch on television or the Internet, and where we go can all affect what our mind is focused on. Staying in God's Word provides guidance for what Christians can keep off their minds. *Put to death, therefore, whatever belongs to your earthly nature: sexual immorality, impurity, lust, evil desires and greed, which is idolatry. Colossians 3:5* Christians can fix their minds on Christ's love to avoid the temptation of earthly desires.

Our bodies are gifts from God that are intricately made. *I praise you because I am fearfully and wonderfully made; your works are wonderful, I know that full well. Psalm 139:14* The complexity of a single cell is astonishing and proof that creation was not an accident. God created the world and all that is in it.

Since our bodies are gifts from God, this should affect how we use and take care of our bodies. In response to God's love Christians should use their bodies to honor God. *Do you not know that your body is a temple of the Holy Spirit, who is in you, whom you have received from God? You are not your own; you were bought at a price. Therefore honor God with your body. 1 Corinthians 7:19-20* God has claimed us as His own. Christ paid our debt to sin by His death and resurrection. When Christians make decisions about how to take care of their body, what to eat, and what they choose to do with their body they should make sure that they are honoring God.

God offers rest for our bodies, calmness for our mind, and His love for our motivation in life. *I lie down and sleep; I wake again, because the Lord sustains me. Psalm 3:5* Christians can rely on the Holy Spirit to provide direction and encouragement. *Since we live by the Spirit, let us keep in step with the Spirit. Galatians 5:25* When we listen to the Holy Spirit in our lives then our minds and bodies will have rest and reassurance.

Taking care of our bodies can bring us closer to God. When we follow what He would want us to do in our lives; we will have more energy and be able to handle all that life has to offer. Christians can be life long learners. God has many things that He can teach us our whole lives about our relationship with Him, His creation, and our relationships with others.

Number 1: Be a good listener

Communication needs to be a two-way street for it to help relationships grow. If all we are doing is talking and not listening then we will miss out on a lot that God has to offer. Christians can talk to God through prayer. God communicates with us through His Word in the Bible and by conversations with other Christians. God's Word can continue to teach us things our whole life. It is a valuable practice to be able to take time and reflect on a day and learn from it's events. God wants to be able to communicate with us throughout the whole day. Keeping Bible verses in your pocket is one way to continue to listen to God as the day moves forward.

Taking time to listen to others helps grow our relationships with the body of Christ as well. *Plans fail for lack of counsel, but with many advisers they succeed. Proverbs 15:22* God puts others in our life for a reason. They might have advice that we need even if we do not want to hear it. Christian friends or family can help make decisions easier and can impart wisdom in many situations.

If people are unsure of a decision in their life or the direction it is going; others can be a trusted source of help. In the Bible there are many incidences where God sends someone to give a message or advice to another. Moses spoke often to the Israelites with messages from God. There is a long list of prophets in the Bible that God sends;

Abraham, Amos, Daniel, Deborah, Elijah, Elisha, Ezekiel, Haggai, Gideon, Isaiah, Hosea, Jeremiah, and Samuel just to name a few.

Listening to others for advice and studying Scripture for God's guidance is valuable but it is important to watch out for misleading advice. The advice from Proverbs 15:22 of having many advisers can help to clear up any confusion. There are those who may wish to mislead people or have their own desires at heart. *In their greed these teachers will exploit you with stories they have made up. Their condemnation has long been hanging over them, and their destruction has not been sleeping. 2 Peter 2:3* This is another reason Christian fellowship is so important. If the only people Christians seeks advice from are not Christian, Christians will have a hard time seeing God's direction for their life. By listening to other Christians you will grow in your relationship with God by hearing how their lives are impacted by their relationship with God.

Being a good listener to others might be exactly what someone else needs in their life. A lot of people are going through life weighed down with sadness. Someone taking the time to listen to what they have to say may make a world of difference. It is hard to really know what another person is going through unless a person takes the time to listen.

Christians can listen to God as well to stay focused on Him amidst the busyness of a day. Sometimes silence and calm is needed during the day when it seems like everything is going wrong. When the stress of a day is becoming too much, listening to God can provide comfort. *Be still before the Lord and wait patiently for him; do not fret when men succeed in their ways, when they carry out their wicked schemes. Psalm 37:7* I have found that taking time during the day to be still and have quiet time to meditate on the Bible verses in my pocket can be a daily blessing. I can listen to God and carry His wisdom with me through the day.

If Christians take the time to listen to others they may find that it will be exactly what they need to hear. Also, someone may have needed a chance to speak their mind. The more Christians live in the moment and do not get caught up in the fast pace of life the more they can realize that God is putting people and situations in their life for them to make a difference. Think of someone in your life that you feel might need someone to talk to and make it a point to listen to him or her. Try just asking them questions and seeing what they have to say. Above all things make sure to take time to listen to God each day so that the Holy Spirit may work in your life and that God's love would show in all of your decisions.

Conclusion: The Word is Life

In the beginning was the Word, and the Word was with God, and the Word was God. In him was life, and that life was the light of men. John 1:1,4

I do this simply by keeping my attention on God and by being generally and lovingly aware of Him. This could be called practicing the presence of God moment by moment, or to put it better, a silent, secret and nearly unbroken conversation of the soul with God.
Brother Lawrence

God's Word provides identity, security, and meaning in the life of a Christian. God's Word is not just for when Christians need guidance, but should be for our whole life. When we study and hear God's Word in its various forms the Holy Spirit can work through us to show God's love to others. When we let the Word of Christ dwell in us richly we are provided with comfort, hope, and joy.

What motivates you in life? It may be a person, a passion, or a purpose. Technology is increasingly becoming more popular as an answer to this question. Technological innovations have helped to motivate and inspire people. Cell phones that allow people to share pictures, videos, texts, and tweets help to encourage and enlighten people's days. The ability to create is enhanced by technology. People can edit their own video clips and songs.

Technology also allows for people to connect with others around the world and to share their passions.

Everyday the world becomes more technologically based. One technology increasing in popularity is E book readers. Some of you may be reading this book on an E book reader. They are digital devices that can hold thousands of books. The days of cluttered bookshelves are coming to an end.

When I was walking through the mall I saw a poster for an E book reader that made me think about my motivation for life. The poster read, "Take your stories with you wherever you go."

Christians know that they are motivated by God's love in their life. The poster made me think of the Bible verses in my pocket. I take God's Word with me wherever I go. As I go throughout my day, I am reminded of how God is with me in my whole life. My faith in God is not something that I only have with me in certain places. It is my life. By staying in God's Word I know that it will be in my heart and mind. Not only will I be taking my faith with me wherever I go; I will be more prepared to share this with others.

The stories that I can share with others are about what God is doing in my life, how God is speaking to me through His Word, and how God has spoken to me through others. Christian Author Lee Strobel notes the importance of stories in discussing faith with young adults today. "Stories are very important because Jesus told stories, and people respond to them." "It's more about sharing why you believe, asking what questions people have, and genuinely listening."[1] Stories that are shared and discussed can allow relationships to be formed with others for the gospel message to be shared. What is the point of taking your stories with you wherever you go if you are not going to read them or talk about them with others?

Identity, Security, and Meaning in God's Word

People that are without God's love as motivation for their life are going through life incomplete. In place of God's love people use worldly things as the motivation for their life. This can lead to people constantly feeling unsatisfied. Not many people can live up to the image of the rich and famous that is portrayed in the media.

On the news I saw an interview with a reality television star who had recently undergone 16 hours of plastic surgery that involved ten different operations. The interviewer asked her what message she would give to young girls who viewed her as a role model. The reality television star responded, "I would just want young girls to know that what is on the inside is the most important." This response demonstrates the conflicting messages that can be portrayed in the media that can lead people to have feelings of inadequacy.

Morrie Schwartz[v] also noticed that the world sometimes makes us feel that we are not good enough. "The culture we have does not make people feel good about themselves. And you have to be strong enough to say if the culture doesn't work, don't buy it."

If our main relationship is with God then we know that our worth comes from God. Living in His love allows believers to know that they are special and are able to show this love in relationships with others. Simply drifting through life is not what God has called us to do. Benjamin Franklin once commented on how some people stop living life and simply get through each day. "Many men die at twenty-five and aren't buried until they are seventy-five." God wants us to have life and live it to the fullest in our time on earth with His Word as our guide and direction.

Living life for Christ is not always easy, but God calls us to not just drift through life but to stand up for our beliefs. One of the professors in a class that I took at the University of Minnesota said that the problem with younger generations is that people do not have deep enough convictions to say what is on their mind. There is too much of a culture that what others are doing is not what I believe in, but I am okay with that. People need to be willing to speak up for what they believe and have more discussions with others with differing beliefs. The discussions do not have to be done in an argumentative or mean way but in a respectful way in which greater understanding can be built which can allow the Holy Spirit to work in the lives of others. *Let your conversation be always full of grace. Colossians 4:6a*

It can be easy to take for granted the freedom of religion that many of us have enjoyed. It shows the power of God when those that are faced with great adversity do not relinquish their beliefs. When the Holy Spirit works in our lives we can see everything in the context of our relationship with God.

An example of this is the amazing story of how Marina Nemat's faith in God sustained her during the difficult trials in her life. Nemat was born in Iran and is a Christian. She writes about how her faith in God has been her strong foundation throughout life in her book, *The Prisoner of Tehran*. Nemat was tortured and put in jail for wanting to get an education that was not based on political propaganda. In school she asked the calculus teacher to teach calculus and not politics and was labeled an instigator by the government. Nemat was saved from death by firing squad by one of the guards of the prison.

The guard that saved her forced her to marry him and convert to Islam or he would harm her family. Marina wondered, "Why had he chosen me? I was the embodiment of everything he stood against: I was a Christian, an antirevolutionary, and a prisoner." Marina wondered why she was still alive, while some of her friends lives had not been spared. However, Marina's faith in God did not waver. "My faith in God had given me hope. It helped me believe in goodness despite all the evil that surrounded me."[2] Marina was able to convince her husband to quit his job at the prison; but because of this, he was killed by those who questioned his motives. After this Marina managed to leave Iran with the help of her husband's family and now lives in Canada.

Marina came to the University of Minnesota to give a talk about her book and her life. She is a powerful speaker and her firm belief in God comes shining through when she speaks. In prison she described how she relied on Jesus, because He also suffered on earth and knew what she was going through. Jesus wants to help us in our lives. Marina knew more about the Koran than the Bible and when people in Iran would ask why she was a Christian, she responded, "Jesus was somehow much closer to my heart; he felt like home."

She talked about the importance of young people today to continue to share the love of Christ with others and to work for positive change in the world. She said that if you want to change the world, you have to go and talk to high school students. They are the future; they are going to be the leaders and decision makers. With advances in technology leaders are developing at younger and younger ages. Things change so quickly that education prepares young people for success sooner and makes them more efficient and adaptable. Marina's story demonstrates the importance of youth speaking up for what they believe.

Through God's Word in baptism Christians are called to a new life in Christ. No matter what our life circumstances, Christians know that in Christ they are victorious. Jesus death on the cross and resurrection defeated death and the devil. He paid the ultimate sacrifice for us so that we could all share in the victory.

Because of this Christians can share this good news with others. When we are focused on God and let Him rule our lives, than Christ-like decisions and actions will flow from us as naturally as breathing, even in the face of adversity. We will love and serve others because, in Christ, that is what we are made to do.

At the beginning of the book I focused on the problem of too many young adults forgetting what God had done for them in their lives and not living as Christ would desire. The solution to this problem starts with each individual trusting in God by the power of the Holy Spirit working through the **Word**. *How can a young person keep his way pure? By living according to your **word**. Psalm 119:9* On our own we cannot live a pure life. However, empowered by the Holy Spirit we can follow Jesus example.

The story of Jesus at the home of Martha and Mary in Luke 10:38-42 describes the importance of listening to Jesus. Verse 40 describes how Martha is so busy with all of the tasks in life that she misses out on the point of spending time with Jesus. Martha becomes upset that Mary is not helping her but sitting at the feet of Jesus and listening to him. Martha tells Jesus to do something about this. Jesus sets her straight by saying that, "only one thing is needed. Mary has chosen what is better."

When we take the time to listen to God throughout our day, it does not mean that we will have less to do or less problems. However, it does mean that everything in life will be focused on God's love. All of the issues of life will be put into perspective knowing that God has called us to be His own. Because of this the Holy Spirit dwells within us making us saints in the sight of God. Praise be to God!

In response to God's love Christians can be open about their faith and proud of the amazing things that God is accomplishing in their lives. There are many young adults in the world that are living out their faith. It is important for Christians to keep sharing how God is speaking to them and the amazing things that God is accomplishing. Young adults that are committed to Jesus can let their light shine to others so that Non-Christians do not have a view of Christianity that is the opposite of what life in Christ is like.

I would love to hear your story of how God's Word is speaking to you in your life. If there is a Bible verse that has been meaningful in your life for an event or period of time, share your story with others. If you have shared a Bible verse with someone else and saw the impact it had on the person, share your story with others. Talk to a friend, family member, co-worker, or a complete stranger. Tell them about the great love that Christ offers.

Temple's of God

The devastation of the 2010 Haiti earthquake shook the entire world. The 7.0 magnitude earthquake claimed nearly a quarter of a million lives, injured even more, and left 1,000,000 people homeless. Haiti is the poorest country in the Western Hemisphere and needed an outpouring of support after the earthquake. Many individuals, countries, and organizations offered their resources and prayers.

One organization that worked to help the people of Haiti was the The Haiti Mission Project. For ten years the organization has felt the call to make a difference in the lives of the people in Haiti through partnering with the local Christian church. They have helped to restore one of the few Christian schools in Port Au Prince, delivered hundreds of supplies, started construction on a second church site, and helped with the construction of a building that would serve as an orphanage, health clinic, and food storage.[3] Those involved with the Haiti Mission Project have spread God's love to many Haitian people.

Several people that I attended college with are a part of this non-profit organization. They are great examples of young people that are investing their time, talents, and resources to spread the Gospel message to those in need. When Christians meditate daily on God's Word it will lead them to become more aware of the needs of others and realize that with God's power they can make a difference.

Shortly after the earthquake in Haiti, I was paging through a hymnal looking for a new hymn that I could play on the piano. I came across the hymn "Built on the Rock the Church doth Stand" by Nicolai F.S. Grundtvig. As I was reading through the hymn stanzas it made me think how relevant it's message was to what was happening in Haiti. Though buildings had fallen, people had died, and many were suffering hope was not lost.

Built on the Rock the Church doth stand,
Even when steeples are falling;
Crumbled have spires in every land,
Bells still are chiming and calling,
Calling the young and old to rest,
But above all the soul distrest,
Longing for rest everlasting.

Surely in temples made with hands,
God, the Most High, is not dwelling;
High above earth His temple stands,
All earthly temples excelling.
Yet He who heav'ns cannot contain
Chose to abide on earth with men,
Built in our bodies His temple.

We are God's house of living stones,
Builded for His habitation;
He through baptismal grace us owns
Heirs of His wondrous salvation.
Were we but two His name to tell,
Yet He would deign with us to dwell,
With all His grace and His favor.[4]

God does not need buildings as a dwelling place to be present in our cities and countries. God accomplishes His work through Christians. The Holy Spirit dwells inside all Christians and guides us through our lives. When others are suffering Christians can offer peace through their service. When others are in pain Christians can offer support through God's Word. When others are in need Christians can offer their time and resources. When others need hope Christians can share God's love through His Gospel message.

Through God's grace in baptism, Christians are saved. Then they can share the news of this saving grace with others. God's Word is not just for part of our life, for Christians it is our life. Christians can live and breathe God's Word in their conversations and through their actions.

There is comfort even when buildings and our possessions are destroyed; God is not shaken and is still with us. Help is still needed in Haiti and will be for awhile to come. Recent earthquakes in Chile, New Zealand, Australia, and Japan as well have left many in need of support and prayers. If you have felt the call to volunteer your time and resources, now may be the time.

Living God's Word

Christian adults can have a large impact on young people's lives and the choices that they make. In my life my parents, relatives, teachers, pastors, and coaches have all helped to shape who I am today. When young people are able to have adults as Christian role models in their life it can help guide them as they grow up. The following is one story of a man that tried his best to be a role model for his family, the young men that he coached, and for the town that he lived in.

Ed Thomas was the high school football coach in Parkersburg, Iowa for 37 years but was much more to the town than just a coach. In May of 2008 a tornado destroyed the small town of Parkersburg, Iowa. Ed Thomas led the rebuilding efforts with a dogged determination to return the town to normalcy. Ed was led by his faith. That was what drove his whole life. And that is what got him through any situation. A little over a year after the tornado the Aplington-Parkersburg Falcon football team was able to start their season on the field that was once covered in glass and debris on national television. It was a much needed celebration for a town that was still working hard to finish rebuilding.

Ed Thomas cared about faith, family, and falcon football; in that order. Ed tried to instill in his players life lessons that went beyond football.[5] "I talk about leaders setting an example, the responsibility of being a leader, and the idea of being a servant and a giver. I talk about standing up to do what is right when nobody else will" "There are so many things they can learn from being a part of our team that will help them be successful later in life as a father, member of a church, or member of the community. There are so many intangibles we can teach that they can take with them."[6] He was successful at what he did on the football field and in guiding young men. Ed coached the high school to two state championships and was the NFL's (National Football League) national high school coach of the year in 2005.

However, no one was prepared for the tragedy that would occur in 2009. Ed was supervising summer workouts in the high schools weight room. One of Thomas's former players, Mark Becker walked into the weight room. Becker was suffering from mental illness. Becker walked up to Thomas and shot and killed him.

The people of the town were in shock. They could not make any sense out of the situation. However, Ed Thomas's family showed that Ed's guidance through the years was still having an impact.

Shortly after the tragedy Ed's son Todd showed God's love to the Becker family. "We need to pray for the Beckers too. They need just as much support as we do."[5] The Thomas family knew that the Beckers would be worried about how others in the town would treat them. Amidst their time of mourning the Thomas family lead the way to show that there would be an outpouring of support.

The Thomas family forgave Mark Becker and tried to help his family. The people of the town followed their example. The people of Parkersburg, Iowa also forgave Mark Becker. As the town had done in the past they were able to support each other in the midst of tragedy.

Many might be shocked at how a family and a town could pull together and still support the Beckers. Their son had killed the man who was an icon in the town. Todd Thomas described how it was possible to offer forgiveness and support. Todd commented that if we did not live out what we believe, then what is the point of it all.

Ed's sons Todd and Aaron were able to continue to lead not only with their words but by example as well. Ed's son Todd now helps coach the high school football team. Mark Becker's brother is on the team and is treated like any of the other team members. Ed's sons live their life with their faith at the forefront as they had learned from their Dad.

The Thomas family started the Ed Thomas Foundation to minister to young adults by providing scholarships, resources, and spreading the message of God's Word. Young adults should have trusted Christians in their life that they can look to for guidance and to serve as role models. There can be many negative influences in life. It is important that young adults are able to see how life can be lived with God's Word as the motivation and purpose.

Let the Word of Christ Dwell in you Richly

A Christian's relationship with God is too important to fall out of sight and out of mind. By staying in God's Word we can listen to what God wants to teach us and grow in our relationship with Him. We can come to realize that God's Word is Life and Christians are God's messengers. By the power of God we are made righteous and capable of living out our faith by sharing God's love with others. God's love and ultimate victory can stay in our minds throughout the day and affect our relationships with others.

I would challenge everyone to talk to someone that you would not usually talk with about your faith or what a Bible verse means to you. There are plenty of people that need to hear about God. Staying in God's Word daily can provide guidance for how to serve and witness to others. I know that nothing is more important than for me to let God's love live in me and be me.

Reading the Bible daily and reflecting on God's Word can cause rejoicing or hope in all circumstances. Even in defeat we can learn more about what God is teaching us. If people feel that there is not enough joy or hope in their life, they can focus their life on the joy and hope that comes from God's love. If people feel that their life is lacking purpose, God's Word can provide direction. If people feel lonely, God wants to talk to them through His Word. If people feel discouraged, God's Word offers encouragement. If people feel exhausted, God's Word provides renewal. If people feel angry, God's Word can bring calm and peace. If people feel joy, God rejoices with them.

If people feel broken down by the world or by the circumstances of their life then there is someone that has perfect love for them and wants to have a relationship with them. It will be the most important relationship of their life and will impact the rest of their life as well. Jesus has sought us when we were strangers and rescued us from danger by the sacrifice of His precious blood.

The hymn "Come, Thou Fount of Every Blessing" was composed by Robert Robinson when he was twenty-two years old in 1757. Its lyrics give a picture of how a Christian's life is dependent on God's love. A note appears under the hymn in the Concordia Publishing House hymnal supplement about the word Ebenezer.

Ebenezer means "Thus far has the Lord helped us" and was the name given to the stone of remembrance that Samuel raised to

God's glory. God has gained the victory for us, and we now look to a far greater monument recalling our deliverance: the cross.

Come Thou Fount of every blessing
Tune my heart to sing Thy grace;
Streams of mercy, never ceasing,
Call for songs of loudest praise
While the hope of endless glory,
Fills my heart with joy and love.
Teach me ever to adore Thee;
May I still Thy goodness prove.

Here I raise my Ebenezer;
Hither by Thy help I'm come;
And I hope, by Thy good pleasure,
Safely to arrive at home.
Jesus sought me when a stranger,
Wandering from the fold of God;
He, to rescue me from danger,
Interposed His precious blood.

Oh, to grace how great a debtor
Daily I'm constrained to be!
Let that grace now like a fetter,
Bind my wandering heart to Thee.
Prone to wander, Lord, I feel it,
Prone to leave the God I love;
Here's my heart, Oh, take and seal it,
Seal it for Thy courts above.

Oh, that day when freed from sinning,
I shall see Thy lovely face;
Clothed then in the blood washed linen
How I'll sing Thy wondrous grace!
Come, my Lord, no longer tarry,
Take my ransom'd soul away;
Send thine angels soon to carry
Me to realms of endless day.[7]

God has promised to be with us forever and His love will never fail. His relationship with us is based on His love for us. The Bible is God's way of communicating with us and allows the Holy Spirit to work in the lives of believers.

Without God, people are lost and their lives will end in destruction. *They know nothing, they understand nothing. They walk in darkness; all the foundations of the earth are shaken. Psalm 82:5* The psalmist describes that without knowing God's Word, people really understand nothing. A Christians' life can be predicated on the knowledge gained by life in Christ. Christ did not come to make bad people good; He came to make dead people alive. God brings people out of darkness into His glorious light and life.

Jesus has said what a relationship with Him will bring. *Whoever believes and is baptized will be saved, but whoever does not believe will be condemned. Mark 16:16* In the Old Testament Israel believed in the future Savior. *I wait for the Lord, my soul waits, and **in his word I put my hope**. My soul waits for the Lord more than watchmen wait for the morning, more than watchmen wait for the morning. O Israel, put your hope in the Lord, for with the Lord is **unfailing love** and with him is **full redemption**. Psalm 130: 5-7* Jesus has shown his unfailing love by giving himself as a sacrifice for us. Jesus came and redeemed us by dying for our sins to give us life. Christians know that eternal life awaits them in heaven. There is comfort in this message.

The true Gospel message of the Bible is priceless and powerful. Paul, formerly Saul who persecuted the church, knew the power of this priceless message. He felt that a person who would do God's work *must hold firmly to the trustworthy message as it has been taught, so that he can encourage others by sound doctrine and refute those who oppose it. Titus 1:9*

Dwelling on God's Word and living for Christ brings direction, life, love, service to others, and the most important relationship of one's life. God's Word can be trusted and will be around for all time. *And surely I am with you always, to the very end of the age. Matthew 28:20b Heaven and earth will pass away, but my words will never pass away. Matthew 24:35*

Spend time meditating in God's Word and in fellowship with other believers and watch the astonishing things God will do in your life. Keeping Bible verses in my pocket has been one way to keep my relationship with God at the forefront of my life. A Christian's whole life can be put in God's hands. The more time people spend in God's Word the more natural this will become through the power of the Holy Spirit. When one sees God's hand in everything, it is easy to put everything in God's hands.

Paul in his letter to the Colossians sums up what trusting in God can bring in the life of a Christian. Take some time to reflect on these words and put them in your pocket if you like.

Therefore, as God's chosen people, holy and dearly loved, clothe yourselves with compassion, kindness, humility, gentleness and patience. Bear with each other and forgive whatever grievances you may have against one another. Forgive as the Lord forgave you.

And over all these virtues put on love, which binds them all together in perfect unity. Let the peace of Christ rule in you hearts, since as members of one body you were called to peace. And be thankful. Let the word of Christ dwell in you richly as you teach and admonish one another with all wisdom, and as you sing psalms, hymns and spiritual songs with gratitude in your hearts to God. And whatever you do, whether in word or deed, do it all in the name of the Lord Jesus, giving thanks to God the Father through him. Colossians 3:12-17

Bible Verses in Your Pocket

Looking for story submissions!!!

Do you have a story of a special event or moment in your life when someone has shared a Bible verse with you and it impacted your life? Have you shared a Bible verse with someone else and witnessed the impact of God's Word?

The Bible has valuable wisdom to impart for any emotion or situation.

I am looking for stories about a time when a Bible verse(s) had an impact on your life or when you shared a Bible verse with someone else and the impact that it had. Submissions can be up to ten pages. Guidelines for submissions can be viewed at www.bibleversesinmypocket.com.
Christians each have their own individual story of how God has worked in their life. Sharing the experiences of your relationship with God can be a powerful tool for God to work in the lives of others.

If anyone speaks, he should do it as one speaking the very words of God. If anyone serves, he should do it with the strength God provides, so that in all things God may be praised through Jesus Christ. To him be the glory and the power for ever and ever. Amen.
1 Peter 4:11
Email stories to: bibleinyourpocket@me.com

Videos of stories in the book can be viewed at
http://www.youtube.com/user/bvinmypocket
For a daily tweet and short reflection of a Bible Verse find me on twitter @stohlmam
To see my monthly Bible verses that I have kept in my pocket since April 2009, visit my website at www.bibleversesinmypocket.com

Sources

Introduction

1. Norman, B. "Nothing without you" <u>Try.</u> Essential Records, 2004.
2. www.wiseoldsayings.com retrieved August 10th, 2009
3. Jenkins, O. (2001, June 1st). Why elephants never forget. Retrieved August 10th, 2009, from http://orvillejenkins.com/words/elephant.html
4. Davis, J. & Wolf H. (1984) Introduction to Judges. In Barker K., Burdick, D., Stek, J., Wessel W., &Youngblood, R. (Eds.), *Concordia self-study Bible new international version* (pp.324-326). Saint Louis: Concordia publishing house.
5. Newport, F. (2010, June 25th). American's church attendance inches up in 2010. Retrieved July 6th, 2010 from http://www.gallup.com/poll/141044/Americans-Church-Attendance-Inches-2010.aspx
6. Grossman, C. (2010, April, 27th). Survey: 72% of millennials 'more spiritual than religious.' *USA Today*. Retrieved July 9th, 2010 from http://www.usatoday.com/news/religion/2010-04-27 1Amillfaith27_ST_N.htm?csp=obnetwork
7. Kinnaman, D. & Lyons, G. (2007). *Unchristian: what a new generation really thinks about*

Christianity…and why it matters. Grand Rapids, MI: Baker Books.

8. Courtney, K & Polich, J. (2009). Binge drinking in young adults: data, definitions, and determinants. *Psychological Bulletin, 135*(1), 142-156.

9. About crohn's disease. Retrieved August 1st, 2009, from http://www.ccfa.org/info/about/crohns Crohn's and Colitis Foundation of America.

10. Bronson, P. (2006, October 23rd). How we spend our leisure time. Retrieved June 26th, 2010, from http://www.time.com/time/nation/article/0,8599,1549394,00.html

11. Time spent watching TV continues growing. (2008, November 25th). Retrieved June 26th, 2010, from http://mediadecoder.blogs.nytimes.com/2008/11/25/time-spent-watching-tv-continues-growing/?scp=2&sq=average%20time%20spent&st=cse

12. Stelter, B. (2009, March 26th). 8 hours a day spent on screens, study finds. Retrieved June 26th, 2010, from http://www.nytimes.com/2009/03/27/business/media/27adco.html?sq=average%20time%20spent&st=cse&adxnnl=1&scp=3&adxnnlx=1277564434-NDwAU3V1FaPVgIB1zjInqQ

13. Sanchez, P. (2000). Waiting and welcoming the coming one. Retrieved June 26th, 2010, from http://www.nationalcatholicreporter.org/sanchez/locked/cyclea/adventa/advent295a.html

Chapter one

1. Wisconsin man celebrates sixty years with same company. (2007, October 30th). Retrieved July 15th 2009, from

http://wcco.com/watercooler/Wisconsin.job.dedication.2.462231.html

2. This section contains insights from a Lenten sermon by Rev. Dean Nadasdy.
3. Stacey, P. "You're not shaken." Into the Light Reunion Records, 2009
4. Gener8xion Entertainment & Crouch, M. (2009). *The Cross.* USA: Gener8xion Entertainment.
5. Gaither, B. "Because he lives." The Bill Gaither Trio: Because He Lives. Provident Music, 1998.

Chapter two

1. U2. "I still haven't found what I'm looking for". The Joshua Tree. Island, 1987.
2. Fairchild, M. (2009). How to avoid temptation. Retrieved October 3rd 2009 from *http://christianity.about.com/od/newchristians/ht/avoidtemptation.htm*
3. Luther, M. (1529). *Luther's small catechism.* St. Louis, MO: Concordia Publishing House.
4. Camp, J. "There will be a day" Speaking loud. BEC recordings, 2008.

Chapter three

1. Warner Bros. Pictures & Reiner, R. (2007). *The Bucket List.* USA. Warner Bros.
2. Ten Boom, C. (1953). *Amazing Love.* Fort Washington, PA: Christian Literature Crusade.
3. The Miniature Earth. Retrieved December 10th, 2009, from http://www.miniature-earth.com.
4. Bell, R. (2005). *Velvet Elvis.* Grand Rapids, MI: Zondervan.

Chapter four

1. Median Age at First Marriage, 1890-2007 (2009). Retrieved May 18th, 2010, from http://www.infoplease.com/ipa/A0005061.html

2. Life Expectancy. (2010, May) Retrieved May 18th, 2010 from http://www.google.com/publicdata?ds=wb-wdi&met=sp_dyn_le00_in&idim=country:USA&dl=en&hl=en&q=average+life+expectancy+united+states

3. Marriage and Divorce: The Statistics. (2009). Retrieved May 18th, 2010, from http://drphil.com/articles/article/351

4. National Marriage and Divorce Rate Trends. (2009, Nov.). Retrieved May 18th, 2010, from http://www.cdc.gov/nchs/nvss/marriage_divorce_tables.htm

5. Kelly Hildebrandt to wed.......... Kelly Hildebrandt? (2009, July). Retrieved January 8th, 2010, from http://today.msnbc.msn.com/id/31994977

6. Foote, B. "You are my king (amazing love)."

7. McGee, J. & DeBernardo, C. (1999). The Classroom Avenger. *The Forensic Examiner, 8*(5 & 6).

8. Thomas, C. & Duszynski, K. (1974). Closeness to parents and the family constellation in a prospective study of five disease states: Suicide, mental illness, malignant tumor, hypertension and coronary heart disease. *John Hopkins Medical Journal, 134*(5), 251-270.

9. McDowell, J. (2009). A fresh apologetic: relationships that transform. In McDowell, S. (Ed). *Apologetics for a New Generation: A Biblical & Culturally Relevant Approach to Talking About God.* (pp. 67). Eugene, OR: Harvest House Publishers.

10. Forgiving the murderer. (2004, June). Retrieved August 1st, 2009, from http://www.rollingstone.com/politics/story/6085540/forgiving_the_murderer
9. Third day. "Born again" <u>Revelation.</u> Essential records, 2008.

Chapter five

1. Rudnick, M. (2010). *Journey into prayer.* St. Louis, MO: Concordia Publishing House.
2. Newsboys. "Real good thing" <u>Going public.</u> Star song, 1994.
3. Stallone, S. <u>Rocky Balboa.</u> Columbia pictures, 2006.
4. Rivers, F. (2007). *Redeeming Love.* Colorado Springs, CO: Multnomah Books.
5. Weiner, E. (2008). *The Geography of Bliss.* New York, NY: Hachette Book Group.
6. Pyrros Dimas. (2009, August 4th). In Wikipedia, The Free Encyclopedia. Retrieved, August 4th, 2009, from http://en.wikipedia.org/wiki/Pyrros_Dimas
7. Luther, M. (1529). *Luther's small catechism.* St. Louis, MO: Concordia Publishing House.
8. Abide with me hymn. (2007, November). Retrieved August 8th, 2009 from http://christianmusic.suite101.com/article.cfm/abide_with_me_hymn#ixzz0M6r0YILh
9. Lyte, H. (1847) "Abide with me."

Chapter six

1. March, D. (1868) "Hark the voice of Jesus calling."
2. Acceptance speech. (1964, December, 10th). Retrieved August 5th, 2009, from

http://nobelprize.org/nobel_prizes/peace/laur
eates/1964/king-acceptance.html
3. Olney, B. (2009, January, 11th). Meyer celebrates
   milestone victory. Retrieved August 6th from
   http://sports.espn.go.com/ncb/columns/story?
   columnist=olney_buster&id=3824898
4. Card, M. "The basin and the towel" Scribbling in
   the Sand: The best of Michael Card: Birdwing
   Music, 2002.
5. Yankoski, M. 2005. *Under the overpass.* Oregon:
   Multnomah Publishing.
6. Pape, E. (2009) Car wash calamity: When a freak
   accident fells an attendant, one customer goes
   into overdrive. *Reader's Digest.* Retrieved from
   http://www.rd.com/your-america-inspiring-
   people-and-stories/car-wash-
   calamity/article163553.html

Chapter seven

1. Brehm, S., Kassin S., & Fein, S. (2005). *Social
   Psychology.* Boston, MA: Houghton Mifflin
   company.
2. Araiza, K. (2010, June 2nd). Newlyweds-to-be
   born in same hospital, same day: couple's moms
   even shared a room in the hospital. Retrieved
   June 2nd, 2010 from
   http://www.nbcphiladelphia.com/news/weird
   /Newlyweds-To-Be-Born-in-Same-Hospital-
   Same-Day-95269569.html?yhp=1
3. How to keep a relationship fresh. Retrieved
   · August 10th, 2009 from
   http://www.wikihow.com/Keep-a-
   Relationship-Fresh
4. Kolb, R. (1993). *The Christian Faith.* (pp. 241) St.
   Louis, MO: Concordia Publishing House.
5. Piper, D & Murphey, C. (2004). *90 Minutes in
   Heaven.* Grand Rapids, MI: Fleming H. Revell.

6. See God today? Retrieved June 3rd, 2010 from http://www.seegodtoday.com

Conclusion

1. Sean, McDowell (Ed). (2009). *Apologetics for a New Generation: A Biblical & Culturally Relevant Approach to Talking About God.* (pp. 55) Eugene, OR: Harvest House Publishers.

2. Nemat, M. (2007). *Prisoner of Tehran: One woman's story of survival inside an Iranian prison.* New York, NY: Free Press.

3. Who we are. Retrieved July 25th, 2010 from http://haitimissionproject.org/page/home.html

4. Grundtvig, N. (1837). "Built on the Rock the Church doth Stand". In *The Lutheran Hymnal* (#467). St. Louis, MO: Concordia Publishing House.

5. Jenkins, L. (2009, July 6th). A good man down. Retrieved July 25th, 2010 from http://sportsillustrated.cnn.com/vault/article/magazine/MAG1157377/1/index.htm

6. Pass the legacy on. Retrieved July 25th, 2010 from http://www.edthomasfamilyfoundation.org/default.aspx

7. Robinson, R. (1757) "Come, thou fount of every blessing". In *Hymnal supplement 98.* (pp. 876) St. Louis, MO: Concordia Publishing House.